Baking the Best of Mary Lee's Desserts

*Recipes from 15 Years of Baking Outrageous
Cupcakes, Cakes, Cookies and More!*

Happy Baking!

ML Montfort

Mary Lee Montfort

Baking the Best of Mary Lee's Desserts
©2021, Mary Lee Montfort

Front cover photo by Anna Grace Photography, LLC

ISBN: 978-1-66781-323-3

Dedication

With sincere thanks to all of my loyal customers during my 15 years of baking as the owner of Mary Lee's Desserts in Vienna, Virginia. You trusted me to bake for your holidays, parties, birthdays, corporate events, galas, and weddings – and the importance of that was never lost on me.

I'm especially grateful to my husband Rick, who never wavered when I started this business and who was my biggest cheerleader and solid support as it grew and expanded. Thank you to my sons, Jack and Nick, who were nine and five years old when I launched Mary Lee's Desserts. They served as my very best taste testers and avid marketers. I loved the fact that, as children, the boys never quite understood what Rick did for a living, but they were so proud that their mom was "the best baker in Vienna". And to my littlest boy, Sparky, who was in the kitchen with me for literally every bake. He kept me company and made every day special.

It is my sincere hope that you will find the recipes included in *Baking the Best of Mary Lee's Desserts* to be a welcome addition to your own. There's nothing like a homemade dessert. It doesn't need to be fancy or complicated to be fabulous! If you start with quality ingredients, use good baking equipment, and follow my recipes as written, I promise you great success in the kitchen! Happy baking!

Mary Lee Montfort
Mary Lee's Desserts

I greatly appreciate the professional photographers who've allowed me to use their pictures of my desserts (and my baking equipment!) as part of this book:

Anna Grace Photography LLC, Rich Kessler Photography, and Len Spoden Photography.

Photo by Anna Grace Photography, LLC

Table of Contents

Baking Tips & Tricks

Make a plan, replace old pantry items, buy name brands, buy high-quality fresh ingredients, and set aside enough time. Do not substitute ingredients. Know your oven.

These may sound like common sense tips but, having talked to many frustrated bakers and having read so many recipe reviews, I know these areas to be pitfalls to less than perfect baking.

Make a Plan

If you are planning on baking, and don't have these items normally on hand, buy your shelf-stable pantry items well ahead of time: all-purpose flour, cake flour, granulated *pure cane* white sugar, confectioners (powdered) sugar, light brown sugar, fresh baking soda and fresh baking powder, regular salt, high-quality vanilla, parchment paper, wax paper, and heavy-duty foil. This will make shopping for your specialty items and fresh ingredients so much less daunting.

Replace Pantry Items

Replace any pantry item that you haven't used in a while (if you can't remember when you bought that vanilla, pitch it!). Baking soda and baking powder must be fresh in order to perform properly - I write a date on both upon opening and then discard after six months. Invest in high-quality ground spices (organic when possible) and discard if their smell is diminished, typically one year after opening. Always check the pull dates on your flour, sugar, and all other odds and ends if you don't bake often. When in doubt, replace!

Buy Name Brands

Brands matter, and you'll see in my recipes that I've named names! (There's a complete list of my preferred brands at the back of this book). Generic and store brands are often not made from the same ingredients as name brands, and thus can lack in both quality and performance. For example, generic sugar is *not* pure cane sugar (it's made from sugar beets) and does not perform the same in baking. You may pay a bit more for name brands, but your baking results will be worth it.

Buy Quality Fresh Ingredients

Use only fresh fruit and berries in season, as the taste is far superior. Buy extra-large eggs that are at least from chickens raised without antibiotics, if not organic. If it is hard to find extra-large, use a combination of jumbo and large eggs to approximate the correct volume (virtually all of my recipes call for XL eggs). Always use whole milk and whole buttermilk, full-fat "regular" sour cream, and full-fat "regular" cream cheese, as baking recipes need the fat content to be their very best in taste and texture. Always bake with unsalted butter so that you control the amount of salt in your baking. Never use margarine or butter substitutes!

Make Time

Homemade desserts take time - from allowing ingredients to get to room temperature, to prepping, baking, cooling, then decorating. It all takes time, but it's so worth it! If you are planning on baking, start early in the day: set your cold ingredients (butter, shortening, and eggs) out for two to three hours to get to room temperature. Then once you start prepping, be present in the moment for the rest of your bake. Cakes, cupcakes, and cookies can be ruined by being left out to cool for too long, easily becoming dry. Icings need to chill before using so that you've got the proper consistency to smooth onto your cake layers or pipe onto cupcakes. Most cakes require a "crumb coat," which involves two coats of icing with an hour in the fridge in between (details to follow in the cake chapter).

If time is an issue, most icings can be made one day before using. Many cookie doughs must be made ahead and chilled before baking, and that often is a blessing! And bar cookies need to be baked the day before serving to "set up" before being cut. Layer cakes and pound cakes often taste better after "aging" for a day or two.

Stick to the Recipe

Unless you are a very experienced baker, do not substitute ingredients! Baking is all about the chemistry! Get the temperature, combination, or fat content of your ingredients incorrect, and your recipe will not turn out. Desserts are a special treat - they are not meant to be "healthy". I never recommend changing recipes to try to make them that way!

Know Your Oven

Each oven is different in terms of actual operating temperature. Know your oven - does it run hot, or do your cooking and baking always take longer than they should? Always preheat your oven well when baking, ideally 15 to 20 minutes *after* the desired temperature has been reached.

Oven rack placement and use make a big difference. Most of my recipes assume the middle rack is being used - this allows for even heat circulation around your baked goods. Do not attempt to bake on multiple racks simultaneously, despite what you may read in other recipes (often expressed in cookie recipes with the note to "rotate pans halfway through baking"). Every time you open your oven door, the temperature drops 15 to 20 degrees, which is counter-productive for a successful bake!

I hope my general baking tips prove helpful. You'll find more baking tips and tricks after the Cupcake, Cake, and Cookie & Bar sections.

Baking Equipment Basics

It is not necessary to buy expensive bakeware, but it is important to replace worn-out pans. This is especially important for metal cookie sheets. If yours are worn, uneven, or thin, then it's time to replace them. I use only professional-grade aluminum 13x18-inch half-sheet baking pans. Mine are rimmed and provide uniform heat distribution. Typically sold in sets of two online, they are not overly expensive, and they will make a huge difference in your cookie and cupcake baking. I do not recommend baking in or on anything made of silicone (Silpat).

I avoid baking in dark pans of any kind, including copper-colored ones. Dark bakeware conducts heat too highly, often resulting in dry and over-baked desserts. Instead, I use Wilton's light-colored non-stick 13x9-inch "oblong" (rectangular) baking pans (sold at grocery stores) for all of my bar cookies. My cake pans are 9x2-inch round aluminum pans with removable bottoms, and you can find these online at restaurant supply stores. I love Farberware's non-stick 9x5-inch loaf pans for my morning treats and pound cakes.

Almost all of my recipes call for a standing mixer (I'm still using the one that was my going-away gift from the Union Bay Café in 1995!), but if you don't have one, you can certainly use a hand-held electric mixer. However, you'll likely need to increase the time it takes to cream, beat, and mix.

Here's a list of fundamental kitchen gadgets that will make baking my recipes a breeze:

- Lots of different sized mixing bowls, some metal

- Wire whisks (one large, one small)

- One or two large rubber spatulas, plus one small

- One or two metal spatulas for cake decorating and for leveling dry ingredients

- Large utility serving spoon

- Sifter for dry ingredients

- Fine-meshed strainers (one large, one small) for sifting confectioners sugar

- Cake tester

- Instant-read thermometer

- Three wire racks (the kind with folding "legs" for good air circulation)

- Small zester

- Set of high-quality metal measuring spoons

- Rounded dry measuring cups (for flour, Crisco, brown sugar, peanut butter, pumpkin)

- Stainless steel measuring cups with long handles (for granulated and confectioners sugar)

- Two 2-cup glass liquid measuring cups

- Inexpensive rotating cake "turntable" for decorating

- Foil-lined 10-inch cardboard cake rounds

- Plastic cake carrier (for covering and storing your cake in the fridge)

- Disposable piping bags, metal decorating tips, and couplers

- Inexpensive food scale

- Small digital timer

CUPCAKES

Boston Cream Cupcakes

Butterfinger Cupcakes

Island Carrot Cupcakes

Luscious Coconut Cupcakes

Creamsicle Cupcakes

Double Chocolate Cupcakes

German Chocolate Cupcakes

Lemon & Fresh Blueberry Cupcakes

Mint Chocolate Cupcakes

Mounds Cupcakes

Oreo Cupcakes

Peanut Butter Chocolate Cupcakes

Pumpkin Spice Cupcakes

Old-Fashioned Vanilla with Chocolate Cupcakes

CUPCAKE ICINGS

Chocolate Sour Cream Icing for Double Chocolate and
Old-Fashioned Vanilla Cupcakes

Luscious Coconut Icing for Luscious Coconut and Mounds Cupcakes

Coconut-Pecan Icing for German Chocolate Cupcakes

Lemon Cream Cheese Icing for Lemon & Fresh Blueberry Cupcakes

Fresh Orange Cream Cheese Icing for Creamsicle and
Island Carrot Cupcakes

Vanilla Cream Cheese Icing for Pumpkin Spice Cupcakes

Cupcake Tips & Tricks

Cake Flour

I love making cupcakes! Mine are known for their delicious taste, delicate texture, and how moist they are. I often use cake flour for my cupcake (and many of my cake) recipes. Cake flour is made from soft winter wheat, is very finely milled, and has less protein (therefore produces less gluten) than regular flour. Contrary to the notion that you can "make" your own cake flour, you cannot. Substitutes using all-purpose flour and another ingredient will not perform the same as actual cake flour. Cupcakes and cakes made with cake flour are amazingly light and have a "fine crumb".

Silver Liners

I bake my cupcakes exclusively inside of Reynolds Kitchens Foil Baking Cups (cupcake liners). They are a bit bigger than their paper counterparts, and they help the cake layer stay really moist. Most of my recipes call for the cupcake liners to be placed directly onto metal baking sheets, and it is important not to overcrowd these. The heat must circulate well for all of the cupcakes to rise and bake evenly. A few of my cupcake batters perform better with the liners placed inside of regular size muffin pans. I've learned this by trial and error and hope you will find those specific instructions helpful when noted.

Watch Your Timing and Temperature

Across the board, published recipes call for baking times that are simply too long. As a rule of thumb, you should always choose the least of the suggested baking times, check your cupcakes quickly, then continue to bake in 30-second increments if necessary.

When baking cupcakes, maintaining your oven temperature is so important. Do not remove one pan and immediately place in the next. As I've mentioned, your oven temperature drops dramatically each time you open the door. I routinely reset my oven after pulling out the first pan and wait for my oven to sound, indicating that my desired temperature is back in full swing, before putting in the next.

Cooling and Icing

Cupcakes can be ruined by being left out too long on cooling racks (the likely culprit behind many dry commercial cupcakes). I allow only 30 minutes of cooling, then lightly cover my cupcakes with a sheet of wax paper until ready to ice. You should always ice your cupcakes the same day that you bake them.

In my opinion, so many brick-and-mortar bakeries over-ice their cupcakes. A great cupcake should have the right balance between the cake layer and the icing - the icing should never overwhelm the cake! If you've jumped ahead to peek at my icing recipes, you'll notice a total absence of buttercreams. I've never been a fan, so my icings are made with butter mixed with cream cheese or sour cream. Delicious!

Boston Cream Cupcakes

One of my personal favorites! These were always very popular during my Cupcake Carousel Specials.

Plan ahead as custard must be made the day before.

Ingredients:

3 cups	Cake flour (Softasilk or Swans Down)
1 Tbs.	Baking powder
½ tsp.	Salt
1 cup (2 sticks)	Unsalted butter (Land O'Lakes pref.), room temp.
2 cups	Domino Sugar
5 XL	Eggs, room temp.
1 Tbs.	Mexican vanilla
1 ⅓ cups	Whole buttermilk, shake well before measuring
2 cups	Whole milk
1 cup	Sugar
3 Tbs.	Cornstarch
¼ tsp.	Salt
3 XL	Egg yolks, room temp.
1 ½ tsps.	Vanilla
⅛ tsp., scant	Lemon extract
1 Tbs.	Unsalted butter, cold
9 oz.	Nestlé Semi-Sweet Chocolate chips
6 ½ Tbs.	Whole milk
4 ½ Tbs.	Unsalted butter, cold
¾ tsp.	Vanilla
1 ½ tsps.	Light corn syrup

Directions:

Day 1: Vanilla Custard:

1. Scald milk in a heavy-bottomed pot over medium-high heat (tiny bubbles will form around the edge). Carefully swirl the pot several times during this process.

2. In a large bowl, vigorously whisk egg yolks by hand, add sugar, and continue to whisk until very light in color and thickened. Add cornstarch and salt and whisk until combined.

3. Using a fork, remove any "skin" from surface of scalded milk; add milk a little at a time into egg mixture, whisking constantly. After three to four small additions, continue to slowly whisk in the rest of the milk until fully incorporated.

4. Wash and dry the pot and add custard base back into it. Whisk over medium heat until thick, being sure to scrape along sides and bottom of pot, until an instant-read thermometer reaches 165 degrees (may take up to 5 minutes). Turn burner to low and cook for an additional 1 minute (do not skip this step!). Off heat, add in butter and both extracts, whisking until smooth.

5. Immediately pour custard into a glass bowl and cover with plastic wrap, pressing directly onto the top. Chill overnight.

Day 2: Cupcakes: **Preheat oven to 350 degrees (355 if oven runs low)**

1. Place foil cupcake liners onto metal baking sheets, 9 to a pan. Sift together dry ingredients. Stir vanilla into the buttermilk.

2. Using a standing mixer with paddle attachment, beat butter until smooth, gradually adding sugar in a steady stream. Cream together for 3 minutes on medium-high until light in color and fluffy. Add eggs one at a time on medium, beating well after each. Scrape bowl and mix briefly.

3. Gradually add dry ingredients by large spoonfuls alternately with buttermilk on low, starting and ending with dry ingredients. Scrape bowl and continue mixing just until fully incorporated; mix batter on low for an additional 10 seconds.

4. Transfer batter into a glass measuring cup to fill cupcake liners ¾'s full. **Bake at 350 for 17-18 minutes** until tester comes out with moist crumbs attached and centers are just set. Move cupcakes immediately to wire racks to cool completely, covering tops lightly with wax paper after 30 minutes.

To Assemble:

Using a small paring knife, cut a good-sized hole in the center of each cupcake, setting the unbroken cut-out next to its corresponding bottom. Using a spoon or pastry bag, fill each hole with cold custard, press the top back on and smooth a little custard to cover the top. Chill cupcakes 1 hour before glazing.

Chocolate Glaze:

1. Melt chocolate chips and milk together in a double boiler or a metal bowl set over a pot of 2-inches of simmering water on medium-low heat; when melted, whisk until smooth. Off heat, whisk in vanilla, corn syrup, and butter. Cool 12 minutes.

2. Pick up each well-chilled cupcake and use a small ladle to pour glaze over the top; tilt the cupcake to encourage glaze to spread evenly and to drip slightly down the sides. Lay cupcakes on wax paper until they finish dripping and can be moved to containers.

Best made only one day ahead, kept chilled in airtight containers or bakery boxes.

Allow cupcakes to stand at room temp. for 30 minutes up to 1 hour or serve chilled.

Makes 15 filled cupcakes (you'll have some plain vanilla cupcakes leftover). Cannot be frozen.

Butterfinger Cupcakes

A riff on my popular Peanut Butter Chocolate Cupcakes! These feature vanilla cake, smooth peanut butter filling, dark chocolate ganache, all topped with chopped Butterfingers. I had one of my favorite Girl Scout cookies in mind when I designed this one!

Ingredients:

3 cups	Cake flour (Softasilk or Swans Down)
1 Tbs.	Baking powder
½ tsp.	Salt
1 cup (2 sticks)	Unsalted butter (Land O'Lakes pref.), room temp.
2 cups	Domino Sugar
5 XL	Eggs, room temp.
1 Tbs.	Mexican vanilla
1 ⅓ cups	Whole buttermilk, shake well before measuring
½ cup (1 stick)	Unsalted butter, very soft
8 oz.	Regular cream cheese (Philadelphia brand pref.), softened
⅔ cup, slightly rounded	Skippy Regular Creamy Peanut Butter
1 tsp.	Vanilla
2 ½ cups, slightly rounded	Domino Confectioners Sugar, sifted
9 oz.	Nestlé Semi-Sweet Chocolate chips
6 ½ Tbs.	Whole milk
4 ½ Tbs.	Unsalted butter, cold
¾ tsp.	Vanilla
1 ½ tsps.	Light corn syrup
One pack	Small Butterfinger Candy Bars, roughly chopped

Directions: Preheat oven to 350 degrees (355 if oven runs low)

Cupcakes:

1. Place foil cupcake liners onto metal baking sheets, 9 to a pan. Sift together dry ingredients. Stir vanilla into the buttermilk.

2. Using a standing mixer with paddle attachment, beat butter until smooth, gradually adding sugar in a steady stream. Cream together for 3 minutes on medium-high until light in color and fluffy. Add eggs one at a time on medium, beating well after each. Scrape bowl and mix briefly.

3. Gradually add dry ingredients by large spoonfuls alternately with buttermilk on low, starting and ending with dry ingredients. Scrape bowl and continue mixing just until fully incorporated; mix batter on low for an additional 10 seconds.

4. Transfer batter into a glass measuring cup to fill cupcake liners ¾'s full. **Bake at 350 for 17-18 minutes** until tester comes out with moist crumbs attached and centers are just set. Move cupcakes immediately to wire racks to cool completely, covering tops lightly with wax paper after 30 minutes.

Peanut Butter Filling: *While cupcakes are baking and cooling, make filling and **chill for 1 hour***.

1. Using a standing mixer with paddle attachment, blend butter and cream cheese together on medium-high. Add peanut butter and continue beating until smooth.

2. Turning mixer to low, add in sifted confectioners sugar by large spoonfuls and beat until thoroughly combined. Add vanilla, scrape bowl well, and mix again briefly. Scoop icing into a bowl and chill 1 hour, covered.

3. Top cooled cupcakes with a generous dollop of peanut butter filling, smoothing with a small metal spatula to the edges of each cupcake.

4. Chill cupcakes for at least 1 hour, covered in an airtight container, before glazing.

Chocolate Glaze:

1. Melt chocolate chips and milk together in a double boiler or a metal bowl set over a pot of 2-inches of simmering water on medium-low heat; when melted, whisk until smooth. Off heat, whisk in vanilla, corn syrup, and butter. Cool 12 minutes.

2. Pick up each well-chilled cupcake and use a small ladle to pour glaze over the top; tilt the cupcake to encourage glaze to spread evenly and to drip slightly down the sides. Immediately top with chopped Butterfingers, glazing and decorating only a few cupcakes at a time. Lay cupcakes on wax paper until they finish dripping and can be moved to containers.

Can be made up to two days ahead, kept chilled in airtight containers or bakery boxes.

Allow cupcakes to stand at room temp. for 1.5-2 hours or serve slightly chilled.

Makes 20 cupcakes (you'll have some plain vanilla cupcakes leftover). Freezing is not recommended.

Island Carrot Cupcakes

These always had a loyal following! The candied ginger, candied walnuts, and Fresh Orange Cream Cheese Icing make them extra special.

Plan ahead as pineapple needs to drain for several hours.

Ingredients:

2 cups	All-purpose flour (Gold Medal pref.)
2 ½ tsps.	Baking powder
½ tsp.	Baking soda
1 tsp.	Salt
3 ½ tsps., slightly rounded	Cinnamon
¼ cup (½ stick)	Unsalted butter (Land O'Lakes pref.), melted
¾ cup	Vegetable oil (Wesson pref.)
4 XL	Eggs, room temp.
2 cups	Domino Sugar
2 tsps.	Mexican vanilla
2 cups, slightly rounded	Organic carrots, peeled, grated, then measured

1 cup	Crushed pineapple (Dole pref.), drained very well
1 cup, scant	Baker's Angel Flake Sweetened Coconut
2 Tbs.	Crystallized ginger, finely chopped

Directions: Preheat oven to 355 degrees

1. Drain entire can of crushed pineapple in a fine-mesh strainer set over a bowl for at least 2 hours before starting. Place foil cupcake liners inside of regular muffin pans. Sift together dry ingredients.

2. In a glass measuring cup, combine melted butter and oil. Grate carrots in a food processor with shredder attachment.

3. In a large bowl, vigorously whisk eggs by hand until foamy, adding sugar in a steady stream, and continue whisking until mixture is light in color and well combined. Whisk in butter/oil and vanilla.

4. Gently whisk in dry ingredients by large spoonfuls until just combined. Then, with a large rubber spatula, fold in one at a time: shredded carrots, coconut, and ginger. Measure out 1 cup of well-drained pineapple and stir this in last.

5. Transfer batter into a glass measuring cup to fill cupcake liners almost to the top. **Bake at 355 for 17-18 minutes** until tester comes out with moist crumbs attached and center is just set. Move pans to wire racks for a few minutes; carefully remove cupcakes from pans to cool completely on racks, covering tops lightly with wax paper after 30 minutes. Frost with Fresh Orange Cream Cheese Icing and top immediately with candied walnuts.

Can be made up to two days ahead, kept chilled in airtight containers or bakery boxes.

Allow cupcakes to stand at room temp. for 1-1.5 hours or serve slightly chilled.

Makes 20-22 cupcakes. These freeze particularly well!

Luscious Coconut Cupcakes

These have always been a family and customer favorite! My coconut cupcakes feature organic coconut milk in both the cake and the icing for a rich coconut flavor throughout.

Ingredients:

3 cups	Cake flour (Softasilk or Swans Down)
1 Tbs.	Baking powder
¾ tsp.	Salt
¾ cup (1 ½ sticks)	Unsalted butter (Land O'Lakes pref.), room temp.
1 ¾ cups	Domino Sugar
4 XL	Eggs, separated, room temp.
1 tsp.	Mexican vanilla
1 tsp.	Coconut extract
¼ tsp.	Cream of tartar
1 14-oz. can	Unsweetened regular coconut milk (Thai Kitchen Organic or similar)
1 ½ 14-oz. bags	Baker's Angel Flake Sweetened Coconut

Directions: *You'll need two standing mixer bowls for this recipe.*

Preheat oven to 350 degrees

1. Chill one standing mixer bowl and whisk attachment in freezer. Place foil cupcake liners onto metal baking sheets, 12 to a pan. Sift together dry ingredients. In a separate small bowl, whisk coconut milk, setting aside ¼ cup for the icing.

2. In the non-chilled bowl, use paddle attachment to beat butter on medium-high until smooth, gradually adding sugar in a steady stream. Cream for 2.5 minutes until light in color and fluffy. Add yolks one at a time on medium, beating well after each; add both extracts, scrape bowl and mix until fully blended.

3. Gradually add dry ingredients by large spoonfuls alternately with coconut milk on low, starting and ending with dry ingredients, until just combined. Scrape bowl and mix briefly.

4. In the chilled bowl, combine eggs whites with cream of tartar. Using whisk attachment, beat on high until medium peaks form (do not overbeat). Using a large rubber spatula, gently fold whites into batter in 3 - 4 additions.

5. Transfer batter into a glass measuring cup to fill cupcake liners ¾'s full. **Bake at 350 for 16-17 minutes** until tester comes out with moist crumbs attached and center is just set. Move cupcakes immediately to wire racks to cool completely, covering tops lightly with wax paper after 30 minutes. Frost with Luscious Coconut Icing and *lots* of coconut.

Can be made up to two days ahead, kept chilled in airtight containers or bakery boxes.

Allow cupcakes to stand at room temp. for 1.5-2 hours or serve slightly chilled.

Makes 24-26 cupcakes. These freeze particularly well!

Creamsicle Cupcakes

These taste just like Creamsicles! I love the combination of my tender vanilla cake with my Fresh Orange Cream Cheese Icing. And unlike all of my other cupcakes, this one calls for lots of icing!

Ingredients:

3 cups	Cake flour (Softasilk or Swans Down)
1 Tbs.	Baking powder
½ tsp.	Salt
1 cup (2 sticks)	Unsalted butter (Land O'Lakes pref.), room temp.
2 cups	Domino Sugar
5 XL	Eggs, room temp.
1 Tbs.	Mexican vanilla
1 ⅓ cups	Whole buttermilk, shake well before measuring

Directions: **Preheat oven to 350 degrees (355 if oven runs low)**

1. Place foil cupcake liners onto metal baking sheets, 9 to a pan. Sift together dry ingredients. Stir vanilla into the buttermilk.

2. Using a standing mixer with paddle attachment, beat butter until smooth, gradually adding sugar in a steady stream. Cream together for 3 minutes on medium-high until light in color and fluffy. Add eggs one at a time on medium, beating well after each. Scrape bowl and mix briefly.

3. Gradually add dry ingredients by large spoonfuls alternately with buttermilk on low, starting and ending with dry ingredients. Scrape bowl and continue mixing just until fully incorporated; mix batter on low for an additional 10 seconds.

4. Transfer batter into a glass measuring cup to fill cupcake liners ¾'s full. **Bake at 350 for 17-18 minutes** until tester comes out with moist crumbs attached and centers are just set. Move cupcakes immediately to wire racks to cool completely, covering tops lightly with wax paper after 30 minutes. Frost with well-chilled Fresh Orange Cream Cheese Icing.

Can be made up to two days ahead, kept chilled in airtight containers or bakery boxes.

Allow cupcakes to stand at room temp. for 1-1.5 hours or serve slightly chilled.

Makes 24-28 cupcakes. Can be frozen in airtight containers.

Double Chocolate Cupcakes

My delicate chocolate cupcake paired with my ultra-smooth Chocolate Sour Cream Icing. Yes, please!

Ingredients:

2 ¼ cups	Cake flour (Softasilk or Swans Down)
⅔ cup	Hershey's Cocoa Powder
1 ¼ tsps.	Baking soda
¼ tsp.	Baking powder
1 tsp.	Salt
¾ cup (1 ½ sticks)	Unsalted butter (Land O'Lakes pref.), just to room temp.
1 ⅔ cups	Domino Sugar
3 XL	Eggs, just to room temp.
1 tsp.	Mexican vanilla
1 ⅓ cups	Water, tepid (90 degrees on instant-read thermometer)

Directions: Preheat oven to 350 degrees (355 if oven runs low)

1. Place foil cupcake liners onto metal baking sheets, 9 to a pan. Sift together dry ingredients.

2. Using a standing mixer with paddle attachment, beat butter until smooth, gradually adding sugar in a steady stream. Cream together for 2.5 minutes on medium-high until light in color and fluffy. Add eggs one at a time on medium, beating well after each; add vanilla. Scrape bowl well and mix again briefly.

3. Gradually add dry ingredients by large spoonfuls alternately with tepid water on low, starting and ending with dry ingredients. Scrape bowl and mix just until fully incorporated. Do not overmix.

4. Transfer batter into a glass measuring cup to fill cupcake liners ⅔'s full (do not overfill). **Bake at 350 for 16-17 minutes** until tester comes out clean and center springs back when lightly touched. Move cupcakes immediately to wire racks to cool completely, covering tops lightly with wax paper after 30 minutes. Frost with well-chilled Chocolate Sour Cream Icing.

Can be made up to two days ahead, kept chilled in airtight containers or bakery boxes.

Allow cupcakes to stand at room temp. for 1.5-2 hours or serve slightly chilled.

Makes 24-28 cupcakes. Can be frozen in airtight containers.

German Chocolate Cupcakes

A personal favorite! Authentic light chocolate cake, classic cooked Coconut-Pecan Icing. You simply cannot find the real thing in a bakery.

Plan ahead as icing must be made the day before.

Ingredients:

4 oz. (1 bar)	Baker's German's Sweet Chocolate, chopped
½ cup	Boiling water (boil first, then measure)
1 tsp.	Mexican vanilla
2 ¼ cups	Cake flour (Softasilk or Swans Down)
1 tsp.	Baking soda
½ tsp.	Salt
1 cup (2 sticks)	Unsalted butter (Land O'Lakes pref.), room temp.
2 cups	Domino Sugar
4 XL	Eggs, separated, room temp.
1 cup	Whole buttermilk, shake well before measuring

Directions: *You'll need two standing mixer bowls for this recipe.*

Preheat oven to 360 degrees

1. In a medium bowl, pour boiling water immediately over chopped chocolate and whisk until melted. Cool slightly, then add vanilla. Sift together dry ingredients.

2. Chill one standing mixer bowl and whisk attachment in freezer. Place foil cupcake liners inside of regular muffin pans.

3. In the non-chilled bowl, use paddle attachment to beat butter until smooth. Gradually add sugar in a steady stream and cream together for 2.5 minutes on medium-high until light in color and fluffy. Add yolks one at a time on medium, beating well after each. Turning mixer to low, pour in chocolate mixture and blend until combined, scrape bowl, and mix briefly.

4. Gradually add dry ingredients by large spoonfuls alternately with buttermilk on low, starting and ending with dry ingredients, until just combined.

5. In the chilled bowl, beat egg whites with whisk attachment on high just until stiff peaks form (do not overbeat!). Use a large rubber spatula to fold whites gently into the chocolate base in 3 - 4 additions until batter is fully blended.

6. Transfer batter into a glass measuring cup to fill cupcake liners ⅔'s full (do not overfill). **Bake at 360 for 16-17 minutes** until tester comes out with moist crumbs attached and center is just set. Allow cupcakes to cool inside pans for a few minutes until you can carefully remove them. Cool completely on racks, covering tops lightly with wax paper after 30 minutes. Frost with Coconut-Pecan Icing.

Can be made up to two days ahead, kept chilled in airtight containers or bakery boxes.

Allow cupcakes to stand at room temp. for 1-1.5 hours or serve slightly chilled.

Makes 22 cupcakes. Freezing is not recommended.

Lemon & Fresh Blueberry Cupcakes

One of my most popular cupcakes! They are delicate, beautiful, and bursting with fresh berries. Both the cake and the icing are bright with lemon flavor from the fresh zest. Delicious!

Ingredients:

2 cups + 5 Tbs.	Cake flour (Softasilk or Swans Down)
2 tsps.	Baking powder
1 tsp.	Salt
1 cup (2 sticks)	Unsalted butter (Land O'Lakes pref.), room temp.
1 ½ cups	Domino Sugar
4 XL	Eggs, room temp.
1 cup	Whole milk
1 Large	Lemon for zesting
2 tsps.	Mexican vanilla
11 oz. (from 2 containers)	Fresh blueberries (use more if berries are large)
1 Tbs.	All-purpose flour for tossing

Directions: **Preheat oven to 350 degrees**

1. In a glass measuring cup, combine milk, lemon zest, and vanilla and steep for at least 45 minutes. Wash blueberries and lay them to dry on paper towels. Place foil cupcake liners onto metal baking sheets, 12 to a pan. Sift together dry ingredients.

2. Using a standing mixer with paddle attachment, beat butter until smooth, gradually adding sugar in a steady stream. Cream together for 2.5 minutes on medium-high until light in color and fluffy. Add eggs one at a time on medium, beating well after each. Scrape bowl and mix until well blended.

3. Gradually add in dry ingredients by large spoonfuls alternating with lemon/milk mixture on low, starting and ending with dry ingredients, until well combined. Scrape bowl and mix briefly (batter may look slightly curdled).

4. Toss blueberries in 1 Tbs. of flour and gently fold into batter using a large rubber spatula, taking care not to break any berries.

5. Transfer batter into a glass measuring cup to fill cupcake liners ¾'s full. **Bake at 350 for 17-18 minutes** until tester comes out clean and center springs back when lightly touched. Move cupcakes immediately to wire racks to cool completely, covering tops lightly with wax paper after 30 minutes. Frost with well-chilled Lemon Cream Cheese Icing.

Can be made up to two days ahead, kept chilled in airtight containers or bakery boxes.

Allow cupcakes to stand at room temp. for 1-1.5 hours or serve slightly chilled.

Makes 24 cupcakes. Can be frozen in airtight containers.

Mint Chocolate Cupcakes

These are one of my absolute favorite cupcakes! They are beautiful, unique, and so delicious. Delicate chocolate cake, snappy mint filling, dark mint ganache.

Ingredients:

2 ¼ cups	Cake flour (Softasilk or Swans Down)
⅔ cup	Hershey's Cocoa Powder
1 ¼ tsps.	Baking soda
¼ tsp.	Baking powder
1 tsp.	Salt
¾ cup (1 ½ sticks)	Unsalted butter (Land O'Lakes pref.), just to room temp.
1 ⅔ cups	Domino Sugar
3 XL	Eggs, just to room temp.
1 tsp.	Mexican vanilla
1 ⅓ cups	Water, tepid (90 degrees on instant-read thermometer)

½ cup (1 stick)	Unsalted butter, very soft
8 oz.	Regular cream cheese (Philadelphia brand pref.), room temp.
2 Tbs., level	Regular sour cream (Breakstone's or similar)
1 tsp.	Peppermint extract
¼ tsp.	Mint extract
½ tsp.	Vanilla
3 cups, rounded	Domino Confectioners Sugar, sifted

9 oz.	Nestlé Semi-Sweet Chocolate chips
6 ½ Tbs.	Whole milk
4 ½ Tbs.	Unsalted butter, cold
¾ tsp.	Peppermint extract
⅛ tsp.	Vanilla
1 ½ tsps.	Light corn syrup

Directions: **Preheat oven to 350 degrees (355 if oven runs low)**

Cupcakes:

1. Place foil cupcake liners onto metal baking sheets, 9 to a pan. Sift together dry ingredients.

2. Using a standing mixer with paddle attachment, beat butter until smooth, gradually adding sugar in a steady stream. Cream together for 2.5 minutes on medium-high until light in color and fluffy. Add eggs one at a time on medium, beating well after each; add vanilla. Scrape bowl well and mix again briefly.

3. Gradually add dry ingredients by large spoonfuls alternately with tepid water on low, starting and ending with dry ingredients. Scrape bowl and mix just until fully incorporated. Do not overmix.

4. Transfer batter into a glass measuring cup to fill cupcake liners ⅔'s full (do not overfill). **Bake at 350 for 16-17 minutes** until tester comes out clean and center springs back when lightly touched. Move cupcakes immediately to wire racks to cool completely, covering tops lightly with wax paper after 30 minutes.

Mint Filling: *While cupcakes are baking and cooling, make filling and **chill for 1.5 hours**.*

1. Using a standing mixer with paddle attachment, blend butter and cream cheese together on medium-high. Add sour cream and continue beating until smooth.

2. Turning mixer to low, add in sifted confectioners sugar by large spoonfuls and beat until thoroughly combined. Add all extracts, scrape bowl well, and mix again briefly. Scoop icing into a bowl and chill 1.5 hours, covered.

3. Top cooled cupcakes with a generous dollop of the mint filling, smoothing with a small metal spatula to the edges of each cupcake.

4. Chill cupcakes for at least 1 hour, covered in an airtight container, before glazing.

Mint Chocolate Glaze:

1. Melt chocolate chips and milk together in a double boiler or a metal bowl set over a pot of 2-inches of simmering water on medium-low heat; when melted, whisk until smooth. Off heat, whisk in extracts, corn syrup, and butter. Cool 12 minutes.

2. Pick up each well-chilled cupcake and use a small ladle to pour glaze over the top; tilt the cupcake to encourage glaze to spread evenly and to drip slightly down the sides. Lay cupcakes on wax paper until they finish dripping and can be moved to containers.

Can be made up to two days ahead, kept chilled in airtight containers or bakery boxes.

Before serving, top each cupcake with a York Mini Peppermint Pattie pressed firmly into the cold ganache.

Allow cupcakes to stand at room temp. for 1.5-2 hours or serve slightly chilled.

Makes 20 cupcakes. Freezing is not recommended.

Mounds Cupcakes

A favorite candy transformed into a favorite cupcake! Luscious Coconut Icing and lots of coconut top these delicate chocolate cupcakes. Always very popular with my customers!

Ingredients:

2 ¼ cups	Cake flour (Softasilk or Swans Down)
⅔ cup	Hershey's Cocoa Powder
1 ¼ tsps.	Baking soda
¼ tsp.	Baking powder
1 tsp.	Salt
¾ cup (1 ½ sticks)	Unsalted butter (Land O'Lakes pref.), just to room temp.
1 ⅔ cups	Domino Sugar
3 XL	Eggs, just to room temp.
1 tsp.	Mexican vanilla
1 ⅓ cups	Water, tepid (90 degrees on instant-read thermometer)
1 ½ 14-oz. bags	Baker's Angel Flake Sweetened Coconut

Directions: **Preheat oven to 350 degrees (355 if oven runs low)**

1. Place foil cupcake liners onto metal baking sheets, 9 to a pan. Sift together dry ingredients.

2. Using a standing mixer with paddle attachment, beat butter until smooth, gradually adding sugar in a steady stream. Cream together for 2.5 minutes on medium-high until light in color and fluffy. Add eggs one at a time on medium, beating well after each; add vanilla. Scrape bowl well and mix again briefly.

3. Gradually add dry ingredients by large spoonfuls alternately with tepid water on low, starting and ending with dry ingredients. Scrape bowl and mix just until fully incorporated. Do not overmix.

4. Transfer batter into a glass measuring cup to fill cupcake liners 2/3's full (do not overfill). **Bake at 350 for 16-17 minutes** until tester comes out clean and center springs back when lightly touched. Move cupcakes immediately to wire racks to cool completely, covering tops lightly with wax paper after 30 minutes. Frost with Luscious Coconut Icing and *lots* of coconut.

Can be made up to two days ahead, kept chilled in airtight containers or bakery boxes.

Before serving, top each cupcake with part of a small Mounds Bar pressed firmly into the cold icing.

Allow cupcakes to stand at room temp. for 1.5-2 hours or serve slightly chilled.

Makes 24-26 cupcakes. Can be frozen in airtight containers.

Oreo Cupcakes

Popular with "kids" of all ages… I had adult customers who requested these for their birthday every year!

Ingredients:

2 ¼ cups	Cake flour (Softasilk or Swans Down)
⅔ cup	Hershey's Cocoa Powder
1 ¼ tsps.	Baking soda
¼ tsp.	Baking powder
1 tsp.	Salt
¾ cup (1 ½ sticks)	Unsalted butter (Land O'Lakes pref.), just to room temp.
1 ⅔ cups	Domino Sugar
3 XL	Eggs, just to room temp.
1 tsp.	Mexican vanilla
1 ⅓ cups	Water, tepid (90 degrees on instant-read thermometer)
½ cup (1 stick)	Unsalted butter, very soft
8 oz.	Regular cream cheese (Philadelphia brand pref.), room temp.
2 Tbs., level	Regular sour cream (Breakstone's or similar)
1 Tbs.	Vanilla
3 cups, rounded	Domino Confectioners Sugar, sifted
9 oz.	Nestlé Semi-Sweet Chocolate chips
6 ½ Tbs.	Whole milk
4 ½ Tbs.	Unsalted butter, cold
¾ tsp.	Vanilla
1 ½ tsps.	Light corn syrup

Directions: **Preheat oven to 350 degrees (355 if oven runs low)**

Cupcakes:

1. Place foil cupcake liners onto metal baking sheets, 9 to a pan. Sift together dry ingredients.

2. Using a standing mixer with paddle attachment, beat butter until smooth, gradually adding sugar in a steady stream. Cream together for 2.5 minutes on medium-high until light in color and fluffy. Add eggs one at a time on medium, beating well after each; add vanilla. Scrape bowl well and mix again briefly.

3. Gradually add dry ingredients by large spoonfuls alternately with tepid water on low, starting and ending with dry ingredients. Scrape bowl and mix just until fully incorporated. Do not overmix.

4. Transfer batter into a glass measuring cup to fill cupcake liners ⅔'s full (do not overfill). **Bake at 350 for 16-17 minutes** until tester comes out clean and center springs back when lightly touched. Move cupcakes immediately to wire racks to cool completely, covering tops lightly with wax paper after 30 minutes.

Vanilla Filling: *While cupcakes are baking and cooling, make filling and **chill for 1.5 hours.***

1. Using a standing mixer with paddle attachment, blend butter and cream cheese together on medium-high. Add sour cream and continue beating until smooth.

2. Turning mixer to low, add in sifted confectioners sugar by large spoonfuls and beat until thoroughly combined. Add vanilla, scrape bowl well, and mix again briefly. Scoop icing into a bowl and chill 1.5 hours, covered.

3. Top cooled cupcakes with a generous dollop of the vanilla filling, smoothing with a small metal spatula to the edges of each cupcake.

4. Chill cupcakes for at least 1 hour, covered in an airtight container, before glazing.

Chocolate Glaze:

1. Melt chocolate chips and milk together in a double boiler or a metal bowl set over a pot of 2-inches of simmering water on medium-low heat; when melted, whisk until smooth. Off heat, whisk in vanilla, corn syrup, and butter. Cool 12 minutes.

2. Pick up each well-chilled cupcake and use a small ladle to pour glaze over the top; tilt the cupcake to encourage glaze to spread evenly and to drip slightly down the sides. Lay cupcakes on wax paper until they finish dripping and can be moved to containers.

Can be made up to two days ahead, kept chilled in airtight containers or bakery boxes.

Before serving, top each cupcake with a Mini Oreo Cookie pressed firmly into the cold ganache.

Allow cupcakes to stand at room temp. for 1.5-2 hours or serve slightly chilled.

Makes 20 cupcakes. Freezing is not recommended.

Peanut Butter Chocolate Cupcakes

Always one of my best sellers and still a family favorite! It's the perfect combination of delicate chocolate cake, super smooth peanut butter filling, and dark chocolate ganache.

Ingredients:

2 ¼ cups	Cake flour (Softasilk or Swans Down)
⅔ cup	Hershey's Cocoa Powder
1 ¼ tsps.	Baking soda
¼ tsp.	Baking powder
1 tsp.	Salt
¾ cup (1 ½ sticks)	Unsalted butter (Land O'Lakes pref.), just to room temp.
1 ⅔ cups	Domino Sugar
3 XL	Eggs, just to room temp.
1 tsp.	Mexican vanilla
1 ⅓ cups	Water, tepid (90 degrees on instant-read thermometer)

½ cup (1 stick)	Unsalted butter, very soft
8 oz.	Regular cream cheese (Philadelphia brand pref.), room temp.
⅔ cup, slightly rounded	Skippy Regular Creamy Peanut Butter
1 tsp.	Mexican vanilla
2 ½ cups, slightly rounded	Domino Confectioners Sugar, sifted

9 oz.	Nestlé Semi-Sweet Chocolate chips
6 ½ Tbs.	Whole milk
4 ½ Tbs.	Unsalted butter, cold
¾ tsp.	Vanilla
1 ½ tsps.	Light corn syrup

Directions: Preheat oven to 350 degrees (355 if oven runs low)

Cupcakes:

1. Place foil cupcake liners onto metal baking sheets, 9 to a pan. Sift together dry ingredients.

2. Using a standing mixer with paddle attachment, beat butter until smooth, gradually adding sugar in a steady stream. Cream together for 2.5 minutes on medium-high until light in color and fluffy. Add eggs one at a time on medium, beating well after each; add vanilla. Scrape bowl well and mix again briefly.

3. Gradually add dry ingredients by large spoonfuls alternately with tepid water on low, starting and ending with dry ingredients. Scrape bowl and mix just until fully incorporated. Do not overmix.

4. Transfer batter into a glass measuring cup to fill cupcake liners ⅔'s full (do not overfill). **Bake at 350 for 16-17 minutes** until tester comes out clean and center springs back when lightly touched. Move cupcakes immediately to wire racks to cool completely, covering tops lightly with wax paper after 30 minutes.

Peanut Butter Filling: *While cupcakes are baking and cooling, make filling and **chill for 1 hour**.*

1. Using a standing mixer with paddle attachment, blend butter and cream cheese together on medium-high. Add peanut butter and continue beating until smooth.

2. Turning mixer to low, add in sifted confectioners sugar by large spoonfuls and beat until thoroughly combined. Add vanilla, scrape bowl well, and mix again briefly. Scoop icing into a bowl and chill 1 hour, covered.

3. Top cooled cupcakes with a generous dollop of peanut butter filling, smoothing with a small metal spatula to the edges of each cupcake.

4. Chill cupcakes for at least 1 hour, covered in an airtight container, before glazing.

Chocolate Glaze:

1. Melt chocolate chips and milk together in a double boiler or a metal bowl set over a pot of 2-inches of simmering water on medium-low heat; when melted, whisk until smooth. Off heat, whisk in vanilla, corn syrup, and butter. Cool 12 minutes.

2. Pick up each well-chilled cupcake and use a small ladle to pour glaze over the top; tilt the cupcake to encourage glaze to spread evenly and to drip slightly down the sides. Lay cupcakes on wax paper until they finish dripping and can be moved to containers.

Can be made up to two days ahead, kept chilled in airtight containers or bakery boxes.
Before serving, top each cupcake with a Reese's "Mini" pressed firmly into the cold ganache.
Allow cupcakes to stand at room temp. for 1.5-2 hours or serve slightly chilled.
Makes 20 cupcakes. Freezing is not recommended.

Photo by Rich Kessler Photography

Pumpkin Spice Cupcakes

These were always super popular during my fall and winter Cupcake Carousel Specials. They are very easy to make and would be lovely any time of year!

Ingredients:

2 cups	All-purpose flour (Gold Medal pref.)
2 tsps.	Baking powder
1 tsp.	Baking soda
½ tsp.	Salt
1 tsp., slightly rounded	Cinnamon
1 tsp., slightly rounded	Nutmeg
½ tsp., slightly rounded	Cloves
¼ cup (½ stick)	Unsalted butter (Land O'Lakes pref.), melted
¾ cup	Vegetable oil (Wesson pref.)
4 XL	Eggs, room temp.
2 cups	Domino Sugar
2 cups, slightly rounded	Libby's Pure Pumpkin (measured from 2 reg. size cans or 1 large)
½ cup	Golden raisins

Directions: **Preheat oven to 350 degrees**

1. Place foil cupcake liners inside of regular muffin pans. Sift together dry ingredients. In a glass measuring cup, combine melted butter and oil.

2. In a large bowl, vigorously whisk eggs by hand until foamy, adding sugar in a steady stream, and continue whisking until mixture is light in color and well combined. Whisk in pumpkin, then butter/oil mixture.

3. Gently whisk in dry ingredients by large spoonfuls until just combined. With a large rubber spatula, fold in raisins.

4. Transfer batter into a glass measuring cup to fill cupcake liners ¾'s full. **Bake at 350 for 17-18 minutes** until tester comes out with moist crumbs attached and center is just set. Move pans to wire racks for a few minutes; carefully remove cupcakes from pans to cool completely on racks, covering tops lightly with wax paper after 30 minutes. Frost with Vanilla Cream Cheese Icing.

Can be made up to two days ahead, kept chilled in airtight containers or bakery boxes.

Allow cupcakes to stand at room temp. for 1-1.5 hours or serve slightly chilled.

Makes 22-23 cupcakes. These freeze well!

Old-Fashioned Vanilla with Chocolate Cupcakes

My moist and tender vanilla cupcake paired with my Chocolate Sour Cream Icing is unbeatable for this classic combination! These were always included on my Cupcake Carousel Specials as they were popular with kids and adults alike!

Ingredients:

3 cups	Cake flour (Softasilk or Swans Down)
1 Tbs.	Baking powder
½ tsp.	Salt
1 cup (2 sticks)	Unsalted butter (Land O'Lakes pref.), room temp.
2 cups	Domino Sugar
5 XL	Eggs, room temp.
1 Tbs.	Mexican vanilla
1 ⅓ cups	Whole buttermilk, shake well before measuring

Directions: **Preheat oven to 350 degrees (355 if oven runs low)**

1. Place foil cupcake liners onto metal baking sheets, 9 to a pan. Sift together dry ingredients. Stir vanilla into the buttermilk.

2. Using a standing mixer with paddle attachment, beat butter until smooth, gradually adding sugar in a steady stream. Cream together for 3 minutes on medium-high until light in color and fluffy. Add eggs one at a time on medium, beating well after each. Scrape bowl and mix briefly.

3. Gradually add dry ingredients by large spoonfuls alternately with buttermilk on low, starting and ending with dry ingredients. Scrape bowl and continue mixing just until fully incorporated; mix batter on low for an additional 10 seconds.

4. Transfer batter into a glass measuring cup to fill cupcake liners ¾'s full. **Bake at 350 for 17-18 minutes** until tester comes out with moist crumbs attached and centers are just set. Move cupcakes immediately to wire racks to cool completely, covering tops lightly with wax paper after 30 minutes. Frost with well-chilled Chocolate Sour Cream Icing.

Can be made up to two days ahead, kept chilled in airtight containers or bakery boxes.

Allow cupcakes to stand at room temp. for 1.5-2 hours or serve slightly chilled.

Makes 24-28 cupcakes. Can be frozen in airtight containers.

Chocolate Sour Cream Icing

for Double Chocolate and Old-Fashioned Vanilla with Chocolate Cupcakes

This will frost 24-28 cupcakes. This icing is exceptionally smooth and luscious and makes for an exceptional cupcake!

Ingredients:

1 ¼ cups (2 ½ sticks)	Unsalted butter (Land O'Lakes pref.), cold cut into pieces
5 oz. (1 ¼ bars)	Ghirardelli's Semi-Sweet Chocolate, chopped
¾ cup + 2 Tbs.	Hershey's Cocoa Powder
1 ½ - 2 Tbs.	Mexican vanilla
4 ⅓ cups, slightly rounded	Domino Confectioners Sugar, sifted
¾ cup + 3 Tbs. (both slightly rounded)	Regular sour cream (Breakstone's or similar)

Directions:

1. Melt butter and chocolate together in a double boiler or a metal bowl set over a pot of 2-inches of simmering water on medium-low heat. When melted, whisk until smooth. Whisk cocoa immediately into warm chocolate and remove from heat to cool slightly.

2. Pour still warm chocolate mixture into a standing mixer bowl. With whisk attachment and mixer on low, gradually add in sifted confectioners sugar by large spoonfuls alternatively with sour cream. Scrape sides and bottom of bowl and beat on medium-high until smooth. Add 1 ½ Tbs. of vanilla, mix and taste, adding more as needed.

3. Chill icing uncovered for 2-2.5 hours, until *very* set and ready to pipe.

Double Chocolate Cupcakes:

Use a medium star tip to pipe icing in a concentric circle, starting at the very edge and working your way to the center.

Old-Fashioned Vanilla with Chocolate Cupcakes:

Use a large star tip and pull straight up with your icing to pipe stars all over.

Cupcakes made with this icing must be refrigerated.

Icing can be made the day before, left out at room temp. 2 hours to soften just enough to pipe.

Luscious Coconut Icing

for Luscious Coconut and Mounds Cupcakes

This will frost 24-28 cupcakes. When making this for Mounds Cupcakes, you'll only be using a little bit from the can of coconut milk, but you can freeze the rest for another use.

Ingredients:

12 oz.	Regular cream cheese (Philadelphia brand pref.), softened
½ cup (1 stick)	Unsalted butter (Land O' Lakes pref.), very soft
5 cups, slightly rounded	Domino Confectioners Sugar, sifted
¼ cup	Regular coconut milk (Thai Kitchen Organic or similar)
¾ tsp.	Mexican vanilla
2 - 3 tsps.	Coconut extract
1 ½ 14-oz. bags	Baker's Angel Flake Sweetened Coconut

Directions:

1. Using a standing mixer with paddle attachment, cream butter and cream cheese together on medium-high until fluffy and well combined.

2. Gradually add in half the sifted confectioners sugar by large spoonfuls with mixer on low; blend in all of the coconut milk, then slowly add the rest of the sugar. Scrape bowl and continue to beat until smooth. Add vanilla and 2 tsps. of the coconut extract, mix and taste the icing, and add more of the coconut extract as needed.

3. Chill icing for 1-1.5 hours covered, until just set and ready to use. The icing should be slightly firm but spreadable. Use a small metal spatula to smooth a generous dollop of icing onto each cupcake, completely covering the top and spreading right to the edge. Frost only a few at a time, then immediately mound coconut on top. Gently press the coconut into the icing with cupped fingers, turning each cupcake as you go. Be generous!

Cupcakes made with this icing must be refrigerated.

Icing can be made the day before, left out at room temp. 2-2.5 hours to soften enough to be spreadable.

Photo credit: Budarinphoto on Creative Market

Coconut-Pecan Icing

for German Chocolate Cupcakes

This will frost one batch of 22 cupcakes.

Plan ahead as the icing must be chilled overnight.

Ingredients:

1 12-oz. can	Evaporated milk (PET or similar)
1 ½ cups, slightly rounded	Domino Sugar
¾ cup (1 ½ sticks)	Unsalted butter (Land O'Lakes pref.), cold, cut into pieces
4 XL	Egg yolks, room temp., slightly beaten
1 ½ tsps.	Mexican vanilla
7 oz.	Baker's Angel Flake Sweetened Coconut
1 ½ cups, slightly rounded	Pecans* (measure first, then chop)

Directions:

1. Have all ingredients prepped and measured before starting. Chop whole pecans fairly fine by pulsing in a food processor (some smallish pieces are ok).

2. Pour evaporated milk into a heavy-bottomed pot and, off heat, whisk in the granulated sugar and lightly beaten eggs yolks; add cold butter.

3. On medium heat, cook the icing for 12-15 minutes. Use a large rubber spatula to constantly stir until thickened and an instant-read thermometer reaches 165 degrees. Do not allow icing to boil. Add vanilla for the last 1 minute of cooking.

4. Off heat, immediately stir in coconut and pecans. Pour icing into a large bowl and cool on the counter, uncovered, for at least 1 hour. Cover tightly with plastic wrap and chill overnight before using. Use a small metal spatula to smooth a relatively small dollop of chilled icing onto each cupcake. Be sure to cover the top well and go right to and include the edges.

---

* When using whole nuts, always place nuts on a large plate and look for any partial shells or discoloration and discard those nuts before chopping.

Cupcakes made with this icing must be refrigerated.

Icing must be made the day before for best results (successfully adhering to the cupcakes!).

Lemon Cream Cheese Icing

for Lemon & Fresh Blueberry Cupcakes

This will frost 24-28 cupcakes. I love to pipe this icing so that the finished cupcakes look like beautiful flowers.

Ingredients:

16 oz.	Regular cream cheese (Philadelphia brand pref.), softened
¾ cup (1 ½ sticks)	Unsalted butter (Land O'Lakes pref.), very soft
4 ½ cups, slightly rounded	Domino Confectioners Sugar, sifted
1 Large	Lemon for zesting
1 tsp.	Mexican vanilla
1 ¼ tsps.	Lemon extract
¼ tsp.	Lemon oil

Directions:

1. Using a standing mixer with paddle attachment, cream butter and cream cheese together on medium-high until somewhat combined. Add fresh zest and continue beating to release the oils, until mixture is fluffy and well blended.

2. Gradually add in sifted confectioners sugar by large spoonfuls with mixer on low; scrape bowl and continue to mix until smooth. Add extracts, mix and taste the icing, and add a tiny bit more of the lemon extract as needed.

3. Chill icing for 1.5-2 hours covered, until *very* set and ready to pipe. Use a pastry bag and two different tips to decorate these cupcakes into a flower petal design. Plain hole tip for the center and medium leaf tip for the petals.

Cupcakes made with this icing must be refrigerated.

Icing can be made the day before, left out at room temp. 2 hours to soften just enough to pipe.

Fresh Orange Cream Cheese Icing

for Island Carrot and Creamsicle Cupcakes

This will frost 24-28 cupcakes. This icing is so bright and fresh tasting. Use an orange that has rough skin to get enough zest!

Ingredients:

16 oz.	Regular cream cheese (Philadelphia brand pref.), softened
¾ cup (1 ½ sticks)	Unsalted butter (Land O'Lakes pref.), very soft
4 ½ cups, slightly rounded	Domino Confectioners Sugar, sifted
1 Large	Orange for zesting
1 tsp.	Mexican vanilla
1 ¼ tsps.	Orange extract

Directions:

1. Using a standing mixer with paddle attachment, cream butter and cream cheese together on medium-high until somewhat combined. Add fresh zest and continue beating to release the oils, until mixture is fluffy and well blended.

2. Gradually add in sifted confectioners sugar by large spoonfuls with mixer on low; scrape bowl and continue mixing until smooth. Add extracts, mix and taste the icing, and add a tiny bit more of the orange extract as needed (it's especially important to get a big "pop" of orange flavor for the Creamsicle Cupcakes!).

3. Chill icing for 1.5-2 hours covered, until *very* set and ready to pipe.

Island Carrot Cupcakes:

Pipe in a concentric circle using a medium star tip. Use a light touch on the amount of icing for this cupcake. Top immediately with candied walnuts*.

Creamsicle Cupcakes:

I use two piping bags to decorate: start with a smallish star tip and pipe a single ring around the very edge of each cupcake. Then use a triple star tip to make a Celtic pattern by looping the icing all around the cupcake, building up as you go. Don't be shy….this cupcake can take a lot of icing!

Candied walnuts: Roughly chop whole walnuts (or buy as chopped); sauté nuts in little butter on low, then add granulated sugar to coat. Stir nuts while browning – be sure not to overcook, as they can burn easily! Finish with a dash of vanilla and cinnamon. Immediately scoop nuts onto a plate and chill uncovered until they have hardened and sugar has crystalized. Can be made two days before, stored in the fridge in an airtight container.

Cupcakes made with this icing must be refrigerated.

Icing can be made the day before, left out at room temp. 2 hours to soften just enough to pipe.

Vanilla Cream Cheese Icing

for Pumpkin Spice Cupcakes

This will frost 24-28 cupcakes. Smooth and classic!

Ingredients:

16 oz.	Regular cream cheese (Philadelphia brand pref.), softened
¾ cup (1 ½ sticks)	Unsalted butter (Land O'Lakes pref.), very soft
4 ½ cups, slightly rounded	Domino Confectioners Sugar, sifted
1 ½ Tbs.	Mexican vanilla

Directions:

1. Using a standing mixer with paddle attachment, cream butter and cream cheese together on medium-high until fluffy and well combined.

2. Gradually add in sifted confectioners sugar by large spoonfuls with mixer on low; scrape bowl and continue to mix until smooth. Add vanilla, mix and taste the icing, and add a bit more as needed.

3. Chill icing for 1.5-2 hours covered, until *very* set and ready to pipe. Use a pastry bag with a triple star tip and pull straight up to create an all-over star pattern.

Cupcakes made with this icing must be refrigerated.

Icing can be made the day before, left out at room temp. 2 hours to soften just enough to pipe.

OLD-FASHIONED LAYER CAKES

Boston Cream Pie

Island Carrot Cake

Luscious Coconut Cake

German Chocolate Cake

Pumpkin Spice Cake

Old-Fashioned Vanilla Cake

MARY LEE'S SIGNATURE CAKES

Devil's Food Layer Cake

Devil's Food Sheet Cake

Fallen Angel

Lemon & Fresh Blueberry Cake

Mint Chocolate Cake

Mounds Cake

Peanut Butter Chocolate Cake

Fresh Pear Cake

Vanilla & Fresh Strawberry Cake

CAKE ICINGS AND ACCOMPANIMENTS

Amaretto Whipped Cream for Fallen Angels

Chocolate Sour Cream Icing for Devil's Food Layer and Old-Fashioned Vanilla Cakes

Chocolate Sour Cream Icing (large batch) for Devil's Food Sheet Cakes

Luscious Coconut Icing for Luscious Coconut and Mounds Cakes

Coconut-Pecan Icing for German Chocolate Cakes

Lemon Cream Cheese Icing for Lemon & Fresh Blueberry Cakes

Lemon Cream Cheese Icing (large batch) for Vanilla & Fresh Strawberry Cakes

Fresh Orange Cream Cheese Icing for Island Carrot Cakes

Vanilla Cream Cheese Icing for Pumpkin Spice and Fresh Pear Cakes

Cake Tips & Tricks

Always remember to set aside enough time to bake a cake - they take the better part of a day, start to finish!

Prepare Your Pans

I always use Crisco to grease the bottoms and sides of my cake pans. Butter tends to over-brown the edges. Cut wax paper rounds for the bottoms of each (tear out three sheets of wax paper, lay over the top of one pan, and cut a circle through all). The wax paper ensures your batter won't leak, and your cakes will remain moist. Peel this off immediately after you flip each layer onto the cooling rack. For springform pans, I use parchment paper.

Ingredients at Room Temperature

You'll see this noted on every single recipe because it's important! For the butter and sugar to cream together properly (thus aerating the batter), the butter must be at room temperature. If you are rushing, you can cut your butter up into fine pieces and let it soften on a plate (do not use a microwave!). Eggs must also be at room temperature for a smooth, fully incorporated batter. I routinely leave butter and eggs out for two to three hours before I start my baking.

Set Timers for Cooling

Always set a timer for cooling your cake layers - too long in the pans or on the racks will greatly dry them out. Most layers need to remain in the pans for ten minutes before being flipped onto wire racks to cool completely. They should then cool for only 30 minutes before you lay a piece of plastic wrap over the top of each, gently tucking a little around the sides, allowing them to cool for an additional 30 minutes before frosting.

Doing a Crumb Coat and Final Icing Layer

The term "crumb coat" was a mystery until I took a cake decorating class before starting my business. Luckily, the instructor explained the what and the why of a crumb coat, and you'll want to learn this for your own cake decorating! A crumb coat refers to the first layer of icing that you put on the sides and top of your cake. This should always be a very thin transparent layer, one which will "catch the crumbs" so that your final layer of icing will be picture-perfect.

Place the first cake layer "dome side" (which is the top of your cake) up or down, depending on the recipe, onto a foil-lined cake board. Then tuck strips of wax paper under that layer. Smooth on a generous dollop of icing, add the next cake layer, more icing, then the final layer of cake. For the crumb coat, use a metal icing spatula to smooth on that see-through veil of icing, completely covering the sides and top of the cake. It's helpful to have a rotating cake turntable for this! Chill your cake for one hour under a cake dome before proceeding. Chilling ensures that your final coat of icing will stick to the crumb coat.

After your cake has thoroughly chilled, smooth the rest of your icing on as you rotate the cake stand. Do this repeatedly until you have the thickness and the look desired. Then, with the help of a metal spatula, carefully remove the wax paper strips. Use the remaining icing to pipe decoratively around the top and bottom edges for a very professional look. If you are new to piping, practice on wax paper before you pipe directly onto your cake.

Serve at Correct Temperature

Cakes should be served at a temperature somewhere between slightly chilled and room temperature for the best taste and texture. Generally, you'll need to plan on pulling your cake out of the refrigerator for three to four hours before serving. I never recommend eating a cold piece of cake. However, I have customers, and my son Nick, who disagree with this notion for their favorite cakes! I've noted recommended times for setting cakes (and cupcakes) out at room temperature before serving on each recipe.

Pivot When Needed

If you have an epic-fail when baking, do not forget that any cake layer can be cut up, placed into a pretty dish or mini dessert cup, then layered with ice cream or homemade custard. Top with a yummy chocolate sauce or fruit - delicious! My friends and family love my Boston Cream Cups, and they can certainly be made with "ugly duckling" cupcakes or less than perfect cake layers!

Boston Cream Pie

Very classic and delicious! 2-layer cake made spectacular with homemade vanilla custard and dark chocolate glaze.

Plan ahead as this cake takes two days to make!

Ingredients:

3 cups	Cake flour (Softasilk or Swans Down)
1 Tbs.	Baking powder
½ tsp.	Salt
1 cup (2 sticks)	Unsalted butter (Land O'Lakes pref.), room temp.
2 cups	Domino Sugar
5 XL	Eggs, room temp.
1 Tbs.	Mexican vanilla
1 ⅓ cups	Whole buttermilk, shake well before measuring
2 cups	Whole milk
1 cup	Sugar
3 Tbs.	Cornstarch
¼ tsp.	Salt
3 XL	Egg yolks, room temp.
1 ½ tsps.	Vanilla
⅛ tsp., scant	Lemon extract
1 Tbs.	Unsalted butter, cold
6 oz.	Nestlé Semi-Sweet Chocolate chips
5 Tbs.	Whole milk
3 Tbs.	Unsalted butter, cold
½ tsp.	Vanilla
1 tsp.	Light corn syrup

Directions:

Day 1: Vanilla Custard:

1. Scald milk in a heavy-bottomed pot over medium-high heat (tiny bubbles will form around the edge). Carefully swirl the pot several times during this process.

2. In a large bowl, vigorously whisk egg yolks by hand, add sugar, and continue to whisk until very light in color and thickened. Add cornstarch and salt and whisk until combined.

3. Using a fork, remove any "skin" from surface of scalded milk; add milk a little at a time into egg mixture, whisking constantly. After three to four small additions, continue to slowly whisk in the rest of the milk until fully incorporated.

4. Wash and dry the pot and add custard base back into it. Whisk over medium heat until thick, being sure to scrape along sides and bottom of pot, until an instant-read thermometer reaches 165 degrees (may take up to 5 minutes). Turn burner to low and cook for an additional 1 minute (do not skip this step!). Off heat, add in butter and both extracts, whisking until smooth.

5. Immediately pour custard into a glass bowl and cover with plastic wrap, pressing directly onto the top. Chill overnight.

Day 2: Cake: Preheat oven to 350 degrees

1. Grease 3 9-inch pans with Crisco, line bottoms with wax paper, dust sides with cake flour. Sift together dry ingredients; stir vanilla into the buttermilk.

2. Using a standing mixer with paddle attachment, beat butter until smooth, gradually adding sugar in a steady stream. Cream together for 3 minutes on medium-high until light in color and fluffy. Add eggs one at a time on medium, beating well after each. Scrape bowl and mix briefly.

3. Gradually add dry ingredients by large spoonfuls alternately with buttermilk on low, starting and ending with dry ingredients. Scrape bowl and continue mixing just until fully incorporated; mix batter on low for an additional 10 seconds.

4. **Bake at 350 for 22-23 minutes** until tester comes out with moist crumbs attached and center is just set. Do not overbake! Cool in pans 10 minutes on wire racks, then turn layers out onto racks, remove wax paper, and cool for 1 hour. Using plastic wrap, cover tops and tuck around sides after 30 minutes. Place first cake layer dome side up on a cake board or very flat serving plate; cut pieces of wax paper to slide all along and barely underneath the cake edges. Fill with most of the custard, add the second cake layer, and finish with a thin layer of custard on top. Chill for 1 to 2 hours under a cake dome. *(Note: you will only use two layers of cake....cut up the third and layer it with ice cream and your favorite sauce for parfaits).*

For Chocolate Glaze:

1. Melt chocolate chips and milk together in a double boiler or a metal bowl set over a pot of 2-inches of simmering water on medium-low heat; when melted, whisk until smooth. Off heat, whisk in vanilla, corn syrup, and butter. Cool 10 minutes.

2. Pour glaze over top of well-chilled cake, using a small rubber spatula to encourage the glaze into a circular pattern on top, allowing it to drip down the sides. Remove wax paper strips. This cake must chill overnight before serving.

Best made only one day ahead, chilled, and brought back to slight room temp. (1-1.5 hours out) or served chilled. Use a serrated knife to cut, if needed. Cannot be frozen.

Island Carrot Cake

A classic reimagined with candied ginger, a cream cheese icing brightened with fresh orange zest and candied walnuts on top.

Plan ahead as pineapple needs to drain for several hours.

Ingredients:

2 cups	All-purpose flour (Gold Medal pref.)
2 ½ tsps.	Baking powder
½ tsp.	Baking soda
1 tsp.	Salt
3 ½ tsps., slightly rounded	Cinnamon
¼ cup (½ stick)	Unsalted butter (Land O'Lakes pref.), melted
¾ cup	Vegetable oil (Wesson pref.)
4 XL	Eggs, room temp.
2 cups	Domino Sugar
2 tsps.	Mexican vanilla

2 cups, slightly rounded	Organic carrots, peeled, grated, then measured
1 cup	Crushed pineapple (Dole pref.), drained very well
1 cup, scant	Baker's Angel Flake Sweetened Coconut
2 Tbs.	Crystallized ginger, finely chopped

Directions: **Preheat oven to 350 degrees**

1. Drain entire can of crushed pineapple in a fine-mesh strainer set over a bowl for at least 2 hours before starting. Grease 3 9-inch pans with Crisco; line bottoms with wax paper. Sift together dry ingredients.

2. In a glass measuring cup, combine melted butter and oil. Grate carrots in a food processor with shredder attachment.

3. In a large bowl, vigorously whisk eggs by hand until foamy, adding sugar in a steady stream, and continue whisking until mixture is light in color and well combined. Whisk in butter/oil and vanilla.

4. Gently whisk in dry ingredients by large spoonfuls until just combined. Then, with a large rubber spatula, fold in one at a time: shredded carrots, coconut, and ginger. Measure out 1 cup of well-drained pineapple and stir this in last.

5. **Bake at 350 for 23-25 minutes** until tester comes out clean and center springs back when lightly touched. Cool in pans 10 minutes on wire racks, then turn layers out onto racks, remove wax paper, and cool for 1 hour. Using plastic wrap, cover tops and tuck around sides after 30 minutes. Frost with Fresh Orange Cream Cheese Icing, dome side down, allowing for a crumb coat. Top final icing layer immediately with candied walnuts (I do this after I've piped my edge design). Chill cake overnight.

Can be made up to two days ahead, chilled, and brought back to room temp. (3- 4 hours out) or served slightly chilled.

Can be frozen in an airtight cake carrier, moved to fridge the day before serving.

Photo by Anna Grace Photography, LLC

Luscious Coconut Cake

A true Southern classic! Dense, moist, and rich, with both the cake and the icing full of coconut flavor. Coconut milk in both makes the difference!

Ingredients:

3 cups	Cake flour (Softasilk or Swans Down)
1 Tbs.	Baking powder
¾ tsp.	Salt
¾ cup (1 ½ sticks)	Unsalted butter (Land O'Lakes pref.), room temp.
1 ¾ cups	Domino Sugar
4 XL	Eggs, separated, room temp.
1 tsp.	Mexican vanilla
1 tsp.	Coconut extract
¼ tsp.	Cream of tartar
1 14-oz. can	Unsweetened regular coconut milk (Thai Kitchen Organic or similar)
1 14-oz. bag	Baker's Angel Flake Sweetened Coconut

Directions: *You'll need two standing mixer bowls for this recipe.*

Preheat oven to 350 degrees

1. Chill one standing mixer bowl and whisk attachment in freezer. Grease 3 9-inch pans with Crisco, line bottoms with wax paper, dust sides with cake flour. Sift together dry ingredients. In a separate small bowl, whisk coconut milk, setting aside ¼ cup for the icing.

2. In the non-chilled bowl, use paddle attachment to beat butter on medium-high until smooth, gradually adding sugar in a steady stream. Cream for 2.5 minutes until light in color and fluffy. Add yolks one at a time on medium, beating well after each; add both extracts, scrape bowl and mix until fully blended.

3. Gradually add dry ingredients by large spoonfuls alternately with coconut milk on low, starting and ending with dry ingredients, until just combined. Scrape bowl and mix briefly.

4. In the chilled bowl, combine eggs whites with cream of tartar. Using whisk attachment on high, beat until medium peaks form (do not overbeat). Then, with a large rubber spatula, gently fold whites into batter in 3 - 4 additions until blended.

5. **Bake at 350 for 21-22 minutes** until tester comes out with moist crumbs attached and center is just set. Cool in pans 10 minutes on wire racks, then turn layers out onto racks, remove wax paper, and cool for 1 hour. Using plastic wrap, cover tops and tuck around sides after 30 minutes. Frost with Luscious Coconut Icing, dome side down, topping each layer, the sides and top with lots of coconut. A crumb coat will avoid the icing pushing out in between the layers but is not absolutely necessary. Chill cake overnight.

Can be made up to two days ahead, chilled, and brought back to room temp. (4-5 hours out).

Can be frozen in an airtight cake carrier, moved to fridge the day before serving.

German Chocolate Cake

My Mom, Lee Hessney Pomponio of Arlington, Virginia, always made this classic for our birthdays! My brothers, Mike, Jim, and Dave, and I always loved it. I've altered her recipe ever so slightly, using cake flour for a lighter texture. This is a beautiful, tall cake – perfect for any special occasion!

Plan ahead as icing is best made the day before.

Ingredients:

4 oz. (1 bar)	Baker's German's Sweet Chocolate, chopped
½ cup	Boiling water (boil first, then measure)
1 tsp.	Mexican vanilla
2 ¼ cups	Cake flour (Softasilk or Swans Down)
1 tsp.	Baking soda
½ tsp.	Salt
1 cup (2 sticks)	Unsalted butter (Land O'Lakes pref.), room temp.
2 cups	Domino Sugar
4 XL	Eggs, separated, room temp.
1 cup	Whole buttermilk, shake well before measuring

Directions: *You'll need two standing mixer bowls for this recipe.*

Preheat oven to 350 degrees

1. In a medium bowl, pour boiling water immediately over chopped chocolate and whisk until melted. Cool slightly, then add vanilla. Sift together dry ingredients.

2. Chill one standing mixer bowl and whisk attachment in freezer. Grease 3 9-inch pans with Crisco, line bottoms with wax paper, dust sides with cake flour.

3. In the non-chilled bowl, use paddle attachment to beat butter until smooth. Gradually add sugar in a steady stream and cream together for 2.5 minutes on medium-high until light in color and fluffy. Add yolks one at a time on medium, beating well after each. Turning mixer to low, pour in chocolate mixture and blend until combined, scrape bowl, and mix briefly.

4. Gradually add dry ingredients by large spoonfuls alternately with buttermilk on low, starting and ending with dry ingredients, until just combined.

5. In the chilled bowl, beat egg whites with whisk attachment on high *just* until stiff peaks form (do not overbeat!). Use a large rubber spatula to fold whites gently into the chocolate base in 3 - 4 additions until batter is fully blended.

6. **Bake at 350 for 24-26 minutes** until tester comes out with moist crumbs attached and center is just set. Cool in pans 10 minutes on wire racks, then turn layers out onto racks, remove wax paper, and cool for 1 hour. Using plastic wrap, cover tops and tuck around sides after 30 minutes. Frost with Coconut-Pecan Icing, dome side down (no crumb coat). Chill cake overnight.

Can be made up to two days ahead, chilled, and brought back to room temp. (4-5 hours out) or served slightly chilled.

Can be frozen in an airtight cake carrier, moved to fridge the day before serving.

Pumpkin Spice Cake

This was one of the first cakes that I made as a young mother for my little son Jack. A wonderfully moist cake, easy to make....it went on to convert many customers who thought that they didn't like pumpkin! My recipe was published in The Washington Post's Food Section in October 2007.

Ingredients:

2 cups	All-purpose flour (Gold Medal pref.)
2 tsps.	Baking powder
1 tsp.	Baking soda
½ tsp.	Salt
1 tsp., slightly rounded	Cinnamon
1 tsp., slightly rounded	Nutmeg
½ tsp., slightly rounded	Cloves
¼ cup (½ stick)	Unsalted butter (Land O'Lakes pref.), melted
¾ cup	Vegetable oil (Wesson pref.)

4 XL	Eggs, room temp.
2 cups	Domino Sugar
2 cups, slightly rounded	Libby's Pure Pumpkin (measured from 2 reg. size cans or 1 large)
½ cup	Golden raisins

Directions: Preheat oven to 350 degrees

1. Grease 3 9-inch pans with Crisco; line bottoms with wax paper. Sift together dry ingredients. In a glass measuring cup, combine melted butter and oil.

2. In a large bowl, vigorously whisk eggs by hand until foamy, adding sugar in a steady stream, and continue whisking until mixture is light in color and well combined. Whisk in pumpkin, then butter/oil mixture.

3. Gently whisk in dry ingredients by large spoonfuls until just combined. With a large rubber spatula, fold in raisins.

4. **Bake at 350 for 22-23 minutes** until just golden, tester comes out clean, and center springs back when lightly touched. Cool in pans 10 minutes on wire racks, then turn layers out onto racks, remove wax paper, and cool for 1 hour. Using plastic wrap, cover tops and tuck around sides after 30 minutes. Frost with Vanilla Cream Cheese Icing, dome side down, allowing for a crumb coat. Chill cake overnight.

Can be made up to two days ahead, chilled, and brought back to room temp. (3-4 hours out) or served slightly chilled.

Can be frozen in an airtight cake carrier, moved to fridge the day before serving.

Old-Fashioned Vanilla Cake with Chocolate Icing

Tender vanilla cake layers, frosted with my Chocolate Sour Cream Icing. This makes a tall, impressive cake. Just right when serving kids and adults! This cake can also be layered with my Vanilla Cream Cheese Icing and candy of your choice (I made a custom Skittles Cake that way for a young customer every year).

Ingredients:

3 cups	Cake flour (Softasilk or Swans Down)
1 Tbs.	Baking powder
½ tsp.	Salt
1 cup (2 sticks)	Unsalted Butter (Land O'Lakes pref.), room temp.
2 cups	Domino Sugar
5 XL	Eggs, room temp.
1 Tbs.	Mexican vanilla
1 ⅓ cups	Whole buttermilk, shake well before measuring

Directions: **Preheat oven to 350 degrees**

1. Grease 3 9-inch pans with Crisco, line bottoms with wax paper, dust sides with cake flour. Sift together dry ingredients; stir vanilla into the buttermilk.

2. Using a standing mixer with paddle attachment, beat butter until smooth, gradually adding sugar in a steady stream. Cream together for 3 minutes on medium-high until light in color and fluffy. Add eggs one at a time on medium, beating well after each. Scrape bowl and mix briefly.

3. Gradually add dry ingredients by large spoonfuls alternately with buttermilk on low, starting and ending with dry ingredients. Scrape bowl and continue mixing just until fully incorporated; mix batter on low for an additional 10 seconds.

4. **Bake at 350 for 22-23 minutes** until tester comes out with moist crumbs attached and center is just set. Do not overbake! Cool in pans 10 minutes on wire racks, then turn layers out onto racks, remove wax paper, and cool for 1 hour. Using plastic wrap, cover tops and tuck around sides after 30 minutes. Frost with Chocolate Sour Cream Icing (for layer cakes) dome side down, allowing for a crumb coat. Chill cake overnight.

Can be made up to two days ahead, chilled, and brought back to room temp. (4-5 hours out) or served slightly chilled.

Can be frozen in an airtight cake carrier, moved to fridge the day before serving.

Photo by Anna Grace Photography, LLC

Devil's Food Layer Cake

This cake was a perennial birthday request from many of my customers (kids and adults). A true old-fashioned Devil's Food cake....unapologetically rich, super moist, set off perfectly with my Chocolate Sour Cream Icing. This is one of my husband Rick's favorites – the icing just does him in!

Ingredients:

3 oz. (from a bar)	Ghirardelli's Semi-Sweet Chocolate, chopped
1 ½ cups	Hot coffee, brewed from:
2 ½ Tbs., slightly rounded	French roast decaf coffee
5 cups	Cold water
¾ tsp.	Mexican vanilla
2 ½ cups	All-purpose flour (Gold Medal pref.)
1 ½ cups	Hershey's Cocoa Powder
3 cups	Domino Sugar

2 tsps.	Baking soda
¾ tsp.	Baking powder
1 ¼ tsps.	Salt
3 XL	Eggs, room temp.
¾ cup	Vegetable oil (Wesson pref.)
1 ½ cups	Whole buttermilk, shake well before measuring

Directions: **Preheat oven to 300 degrees**

1. Brew coffee and immediately pour over chopped chocolate to melt, whisking occasionally. Cool to room temp., then add vanilla. Grease 3 9-inch pans with Crisco, line bottoms with wax paper. Sift together all dry ingredients, including the sugar.

2. Using a standing mixer with whisk attachment, beat eggs on medium-high for 3 minutes, until light in color and thickened. Turning mixer to low, slowly add oil, then buttermilk, ending with chocolate mixture.

3. Switch to paddle attachment and gradually add in dry ingredients by large spoonfuls on low, until just combined. Scrape bowl and mix an additional 10 seconds.

4. **Bake at 300 for 40-43 minutes** until tester comes out with moist crumbs attached and center is just set. Cool in pans 15 minutes on wire racks, then turn layers out onto racks, remove wax paper, and cool for 70 minutes. Using plastic wrap, cover tops and tuck around sides after 35 minutes (layers may collapse slightly). Frost with Chocolate Sour Cream Icing, dome side down, allowing for a crumb coat. Chill cake overnight.

Can be made up to two days ahead, chilled, and brought back to room temp. (4-5 hours out) or served slightly chilled.

Can be frozen in an airtight cake carrier, moved to fridge the day before serving.

Photo credit: Charisse Kenion on Unsplash

Devil's Food Sheet Cake

I made this for many customer celebrations and many a team party for sons Jack and Nick. Jack still requests this sheet cake for every birthday!

Ingredients:

3 oz. (from a bar)	Ghirardelli's Semi-Sweet Chocolate, chopped
1 ½ cups	Hot coffee, brewed from:
2 ½ Tbs., slightly rounded	French roast decaf coffee
5 cups	Cold water
¾ tsp.	Mexican vanilla
2 ½ cups	All-purpose flour (Gold Medal pref.)
1 ½ cups	Hershey's Cocoa Powder
3 cups	Domino Sugar
2 tsps.	Baking soda
¾ tsp.	Baking powder

1 ¼ tsp.	Salt
3 XL	Eggs, room temp.
¾ cup	Vegetable oil (Wesson pref.)
1 ½ cups	Whole buttermilk, shake well before measuring

Directions: **Preheat oven to 300 degrees; use 2nd from bottom rack of oven**

1. Brew coffee and pour immediately over chopped chocolate to melt, whisking occasionally. Cool to room temp., then add vanilla. Grease ¼ sheet pan with Crisco, line with parchment paper. Sift together all dry ingredients, including the sugar.

2. Using a standing mixer with whisk attachment, beat eggs on medium-high for 3 minutes, until light in color and thickened. Turning mixer to low, slowly add oil, then buttermilk, ending with chocolate mixture.

3. Switch to paddle attachment and gradually add in dry ingredients by large spoonfuls on low, until just combined. Scrape bowl and mix an additional 10 seconds.

4. **Bake at 300 for 40-45 minutes,** on 2nd rack from the bottom, until tester comes out with moist crumbs attached and center is just set. Let cool almost entirely in pan on a wire rack (2-2.5 hours). Then very carefully flip cake onto rack; peel off parchment to finish cooling. For a 2-layer sheet cake, make individual batches of this batter and frost with Chocolate Sour Cream Icing (large batch), dome side up. Allow for a crumb coat. For a more casual look, bake one batch, leave cake in pan, and frost with Chocolate Sour Cream Icing for layer cakes. Chill cake overnight.

Can be made up to two days ahead, chilled, and brought back to room temp. (5-6 hours out).

Freezing is not recommended.

Fallen Angel

I first made this cake as a young mother in Seattle. I fell in love with the simplicity of it, and it has stayed an all-time family favorite these many years later.

A single layer French-style cake dusted with powdered sugar: it rises, then falls, creating a lovely, crackled top and a super moist interior. Serve it with my Amaretto Whipped Cream.

Plan ahead as cake must be made the day before serving.

Ingredients:

1 cup (2 sticks)	Unsalted butter (Land O'Lakes pref.), cold, cut into pieces
10 oz.	*Nestlé Semi-Sweet Chocolate chips
5 XL	Eggs, just at room temp.
1 ¼ cups	Domino Sugar
½ tsp.	Mexican vanilla
5 Tbs.	All-purpose flour (Gold Medal pref.)
1 ½ tsps.	Baking powder
¼ tsp.	Salt

Directions: **Preheat oven to 325 degrees; use 2nd from bottom rack of oven**

1. Liberally grease a 10-inch springform pan with Crisco, line bottom with a parchment paper round, smoothing out to remove as many "wrinkles" as possible. Sift together dry ingredients using a small handheld mesh strainer.

2. Melt butter and chocolate together in a double boiler or a metal bowl set over a pot of 2-inches of simmering water on medium-low heat. When melted, whisk until smooth. Off heat, whisk in vanilla, and allow to cool slightly.

3. Using a standing mixer with whisk attachment, beat eggs on medium-high, add sugar in a steady stream, then beat for 2-2.5 minutes until light yellow and thickened. Do not overbeat!

4. Pour mixture into a large bowl. Carefully shake dry ingredients (using the strainer) over the egg mixture, folding gently by hand with a large rubber spatula in 3 - 4 additions. Add still slightly warm chocolate, folding it constantly as you pour it into the base until just fully incorporated. Pour batter into prepared pan and place immediately into the oven on 2nd rack from bottom.

5. **Bake at 325 for 20 minutes**, then lay a piece of heavy-duty foil lightly on top and **bake an additional 30-34 minutes** (cake should be puffed up and just set). Remove cake to wire rack and immediately run a sharp knife around inside edge of pan to loosen; cake will collapse, and top will crack as it cools (thus the "fallen"!). Cool completely on a wire rack (2-2.5 hours); use Press'n Seal and foil to cover tightly.

6. The next day, remove the "collar" from pan and, using a large metal spatula, carefully separate the cake from the parchment paper and springform bottom and lift it onto a large flat serving plate or cake stand. Cut out designs from heavy card stock, lay decoratively on the cake, and dust confectioners (powdered) sugar over them. Carefully remove the paper - you've now got a beautiful stencil on your very chic French cake!

This cake must be stored well wrapped overnight before cutting and serving. Cut fairly small pieces, as it's rich! Serve with a dollop of Amaretto Whipped Cream alongside for the full experience!

Can be stored well-wrapped at room temp. for up to 4 days. Freezing is not recommended.

* Note on the chocolate: I've experimented with different "fancy" chocolates for this cake, and they simply do not work as well. Stick with the recipe as written using Nestlé, and you'll be very pleased!

Lemon & Fresh Blueberry Cake

This was always one of my top sellers! I only made this cake with the freshest U.S.-grown berries, leaving many disappointed customers in the winter months! A very delicate, light, and lemony cake, just bursting with fresh blueberries. Perfectly lovely!

Ingredients:

2 cups + 5 Tbs.	Cake flour (Softasilk or Swans Down)
2 tsps.	Baking powder
1 tsp.	Salt
1 cup (2 sticks)	Unsalted butter (Land O'Lakes pref.), room temp.
1 ½ cups	Domino Sugar
4 XL	Eggs, room temp.
1 cup	Whole milk
1 Large	Lemon for zesting
2 tsps.	Mexican vanilla
9 oz. (from 2 containers)	Fresh blueberries (use more if berries are large)
1 Tbs.	All-purpose flour for tossing

Directions: **Preheat oven to 350 degrees**

1. In a glass measuring cup, combine milk, lemon zest, and vanilla and steep for at least 45 minutes. Wash blueberries and lay them to dry on paper towels.

2. Sift together dry ingredients. Grease 3 9-inch pans with Crisco, line bottoms with wax paper, dust sides with cake flour.

3. Using a standing mixer with paddle attachment, beat butter until smooth, gradually adding sugar in a steady stream. Cream together for 2.5 minutes on medium-high until light in color and fluffy. Add eggs one at a time on medium, beating well after each. Scrape bowl and mix until well blended.

4. Gradually add dry ingredients by large spoonfuls alternating with lemon/milk mixture on low, starting and ending with dry ingredients, until well combined. Scrape bowl and mix briefly (batter may look slightly curdled). Toss blueberries in 1 Tbs. of flour and gently fold into batter using a large rubber spatula, taking care not to break any.

5. **Bake at 350 for 22-23 minutes** until tester comes out clean and center springs back when lightly touched. Cool in pans 10 minutes on wire racks, then turn layers out onto racks, remove wax paper, and cool for 1 hour. Using plastic wrap, cover tops and tuck around sides after 30 minutes. Frost with Lemon Cream Cheese Icing, dome side up, using layer with the fewest berries as the bottom. A crumb coat is a must for this one! Chill cake overnight.

Can be made up to two days ahead, chilled, and brought back to room temp. (2-3 hours out) or served slightly chilled.

Can be frozen in an airtight cake carrier, moved to fridge the day before serving.

Mint Chocolate Cake

This is one of my personal favorites. It's a beautiful cake, lighter than a fully frosted one, and the balance between mint and chocolate is perfect!

Ingredients:

2 ¼ cups	Cake flour (Softasilk or Swans Down)
⅔ cup	Hershey's Cocoa Powder
1 ¼ tsps.	Baking soda
¼ tsp.	Baking powder
1 tsp.	Salt
¾ cup (1 ½ sticks)	Unsalted butter (Land O'Lakes pref.), just to room temp.
1 ⅔ cups	Domino Sugar
3 XL	Eggs, just to room temp.
1 tsp.	Mexican vanilla
1 ⅓ cups	Water, tepid (90 degrees on instant-read thermometer)
½ cup (1 stick)	Unsalted butter, very soft
8 oz.	Regular cream cheese (Philadelphia brand pref.), room temp.
2 Tbs., level	Regular sour cream (Breakstone's or similar)
1 tsp.	Peppermint extract
¼ tsp.	Mint extract
½ tsp.	Vanilla
3 cups, rounded	Domino Confectioners Sugar, sifted
6 oz.	Nestlé Semi-Sweet Chocolate chips
4 Tbs.	Whole milk
1 Tbs.	Crème de Menthe White Liqueur (can omit and increase milk by 1 Tbs. and add ½ tsp. of peppermint extract)
3 Tbs.	Unsalted butter, cold
1 tsp.	Light corn syrup

Directions: **Preheat oven to 350 degrees**

Cake:

1. Grease 3 9-inch pans with Crisco, line bottoms with wax paper, dust sides with cake flour. Sift together dry ingredients.

2. Using a standing mixer with paddle attachment, beat butter until smooth, gradually adding sugar in a steady stream. Cream together for 2.5 minutes on medium-high until light in color and fluffy. Add eggs one at a time on medium, beating well after each; add vanilla. Scrape bowl well and mix again briefly.

3. Gradually add dry ingredients by large spoonfuls alternately with tepid water on low, starting and ending with dry ingredients. Scrape bowl and mix just until fully incorporated. Do not overmix.

4. **Bake at 350 for 16-17 minutes** until tester comes out clean and center springs back when lightly touched. Cool in pans 10 minutes on wire racks, then turn layers out onto racks, remove wax paper, and cool for 1 hour. Using plastic wrap, cover tops and tuck around sides after 30 minutes.

Mint Filling: *While layers are baking and cooling, make filling and **chill for 1.5 hours.***

1. Using a standing mixer with paddle attachment, blend butter and cream cheese together on medium-high. Add sour cream and continue beating until smooth.

2. Turning mixer to low, add in sifted confectioners sugar by large spoonfuls and beat until thoroughly combined. Add all extracts, scrape bowl well, and mix again briefly. Scoop icing into a bowl and chill 1.5 hours, covered.

3. When cake layers are completely cool, place the bottom layer dome side up on a cake board or very flat serving plate; cut pieces of wax paper to slide all along and barely underneath the cake edges. Use most of the filling in between the layers, saving just enough to smooth a thin layer on top. Cover cake with a cake dome and chill 1 hour before glazing.

Mint Chocolate Glaze:

1. Melt chocolate chips and milk together in a double boiler or a metal bowl set over a pot of 2-inches of simmering water on medium-low heat; when melted, whisk until smooth. Off heat, whisk in liqueur (if using) *or* peppermint extract/extra milk, corn syrup, and butter. Cool 10 minutes.

2. Pour glaze over top of well-chilled cake, using a small rubber spatula to encourage the glaze into a circular pattern on top, allowing it to drip down the sides. Remove wax paper strips. Chill cake overnight.

Can be made up to two days ahead, chilled, and brought back to room temp. (2-3 hours out) or can be served slightly chilled. Use a serrated knife to cut, if needed. Freezing is not recommended.

Photo credit: Karolina Grabowska on Pexels

Mounds Cake

This cake takes a bit of work, but the wall of chocolate hugging the delicate chocolate layers, luscious coconut icing, and coconut are so worth it!

Plan ahead as this cake has several steps. You can make the Luscious Coconut Icing the day before to save time!

Ingredients:

2 ¼ cups	Cake flour (Softasilk or Swans Down)
⅔ cup	Hershey's Cocoa Powder
1 ¼ tsps.	Baking soda
¼ tsp.	Baking powder
1 tsp.	Salt
¾ cup (1 ½ sticks)	Unsalted butter (Land O'Lakes pref.), just to room temp.
1 ⅔ cups	Domino Sugar
3 XL	Eggs, just to room temp.
1 tsp.	Mexican vanilla
1 ⅓ cups	Water, tepid (90 degrees on instant-read thermometer)
One batch	Luscious Coconut Icing (you'll have some left)
One batch	Dark chocolate ganache (recipe below)
¾ of 14-oz. bag	Baker's Angel Flake Sweetened Coconut

Directions: **Preheat oven to 350 degrees**

Cake:

1. Grease 3 9-inch pans with Crisco, line bottoms with wax paper, dust sides with cake flour. Sift together dry ingredients.

2. Using a standing mixer with paddle attachment, beat butter until smooth, gradually adding sugar in a steady stream. Cream together for 2.5 minutes on medium-high until light in color and fluffy. Add eggs one at a time on medium, beating well after each; add vanilla. Scrape bowl well and mix again briefly.

3. Gradually add dry ingredients by large spoonfuls alternately with tepid water on low, starting and ending with dry ingredients. Scrape bowl and mix just until fully incorporated. Do not overmix.

4. **Bake at 350 for 16-17 minutes** until tester comes out clean and center springs back when lightly touched. Cool in pans 10 minutes on wire racks, then turn layers out onto racks, remove wax paper, and cool for 1 hour. Using plastic wrap, cover tops and tuck around sides after 30 minutes.

Chocolate Ganache: *While cake is baking and cooling, make ganache and **chill for 1.5 hours.***

6 oz.	Ghirardelli Semi-Sweet Chocolate (from bars or chips)
½ cup	Heavy whipping cream
¼ cup	Whole milk
4 oz.	Nestlé Semi-Sweet Chocolate chips
2 Tbs.	Domino Confectioners Sugar
1 tsp.	Light corn syrup
1 ½ tsps.	Vanilla
1 Tbs.	Unsalted butter, cold

1. In a double boiler or a metal bowl set over a pot of 2-inches of simmering water on medium-low, melt *only* the Ghirardelli chocolate with cream and milk; whisk when melted. Off heat, immediately whisk in Nestlé chocolate chips to "temper" the mixture.

2. Place back onto double boiler over low heat, then whisk in confectioners sugar, corn syrup, vanilla, and butter. Heat briefly to melt butter and fully incorporate sugar. Whisk until smooth.

3. Place in fridge, uncovered, and chill for 1-1.5 hours until firm but spreadable.

To Assemble Cake:

1. When cake layers are completely cool, place the bottom layer dome side up on a cake board or very flat serving plate; cut pieces of wax paper to slide all along and barely underneath the cake edges. Smooth a large dollop of the coconut icing on, then generously sprinkle on coconut. Repeat with 2nd layer, adding more icing and coconut. After placing on 3rd layer, smooth a tiny bit of icing on the top only (do not use on the sides). Cover with a cake dome and chill for 1 hour.

2. Using a metal icing spatula and your cake turntable, smooth about 1/3 of the chilled ganache onto the sides of the cold cake. Return cake to fridge and chill 30 minutes before the final coat of ganache goes on. For the final coat, repeat your strokes until ganache starts to adhere to itself (think of painting a wall!). As you build your "wall of chocolate", be sure to go past the very top of the cake so that you are creating a retaining wall for the last of the coconut icing.

3. Carefully remove wax paper strips along the bottom with the help of a serving spatula. Top cake with the rest of the coconut icing, smoothing to create a nice dome, and then decorate generously with coconut. You can pipe any extra ganache into tiny stars along the bottom edge of the cake. Chill cake overnight.

Can be made up to two days ahead, chilled, and brought back to room temp. (2-3 hours out) or served slightly chilled.

Use a serrated knife to cut through chocolate.

Cannot be frozen.

Peanut Butter Chocolate Cake

My signature cake recipe was published in The Washington Post's Food Section in October 2007 and was always a huge seller for me! It continues to be a family favorite, especially with my youngest son Nick.

Ingredients:

2 ¼ cups	Cake flour (Softasilk or Swans Down)
⅔ cup	Hershey's Cocoa Powder
1 ¼ tsps.	Baking soda
¼ tsp.	Baking powder
1 tsp.	Salt
¾ cup (1 ½ sticks)	Unsalted butter (Land O'Lakes pref.), just to room temp.
1 ⅔ cups	Domino Sugar
3 XL	Eggs, just to room temp.
1 tsp.	Mexican vanilla
1 ⅓ cups	Water, tepid (90 degrees on instant-read thermometer)
½ cup (1 stick)	Unsalted butter, very soft
8 oz.	Regular cream cheese (Philadelphia brand pref.), room temp.
⅔ cup, slightly rounded	Skippy Regular Creamy Peanut Butter
1 tsp.	Vanilla
2 ½ cups, slightly rounded	Domino Confectioners Sugar, sifted
6 oz.	Nestlé Semi-Sweet Chocolate chips
5 Tbs.	Whole milk
3 Tbs.	Unsalted butter, cold
½ tsp.	Vanilla
1 tsp.	Light corn syrup

Directions: Preheat oven to 350 degrees

Cake:

1. Grease 3 9-inch pans with Crisco, line bottoms with wax paper, dust sides with cake flour. Sift together dry ingredients.

2. Using a standing mixer with paddle attachment, beat butter until smooth, gradually adding sugar in a steady stream. Cream together for 2.5 minutes on medium-high until light in color and fluffy. Add eggs one at a time on medium, beating well after each; add vanilla. Scrape bowl well and mix again briefly.

3. Gradually add dry ingredients by large spoonfuls alternately with tepid water on low, starting and ending with dry ingredients. Scrape bowl and mix just until fully incorporated. Do not overmix.

4. **Bake at 350 for 16-17 minutes** until tester comes out clean and center springs back when lightly touched. Cool in pans 10 minutes on wire racks, then turn layers out onto racks, remove wax paper, and cool for 1 hour. Using plastic wrap, cover tops and tuck around sides after 30 minutes.

Peanut Butter Filling: *While layers are baking and cooling, make filling and **chill for 1 hour**.*

1. Using a standing mixer with paddle attachment, blend butter and cream cheese together on medium-high. Add peanut butter and continue beating until smooth.

2. Turning mixer to low, add in sifted confectioners sugar by large spoonfuls and beat until thoroughly combined. Add vanilla, scrape bowl well, and mix again briefly. Scoop icing into a bowl and chill 1 hour, covered.

3. When cake layers are completely cool, place the bottom layer dome side up on a cake board or very flat serving plate; cut pieces of wax paper to slide all along and barely underneath the cake edges. Use most of the filling in between the layers, saving just enough to smooth a thin layer on top. Cover cake with a cake dome and chill 1 hour before glazing.

Chocolate Glaze:

1. Melt chocolate chips and milk together in a double boiler or a metal bowl set over a pot of 2-inches of simmering water on medium-low heat; when melted, whisk until smooth. Off heat, whisk in vanilla, corn syrup, and butter. Cool 10 minutes.

2. Pour glaze over top of well-chilled cake, using a small rubber spatula to encourage the glaze into a circular pattern on top, allowing it to drip down the sides. Remove wax paper strips. Chill cake overnight.

Can be made up to two days ahead, chilled, and brought back to room temp. (2-3 hours out) or can be served slightly chilled. Use a serrated knife to cut, if needed. Freezing is not recommended.

Fresh Pear Cake

A very unique cake, quite adult in taste, perfect for a special dinner party. Only use fresh pears when they are in season, and don't skip the cardamom!

Plan ahead as pears will need several days to ripen at home before using.

Ingredients:

2 cups	All-purpose flour (Gold Medal pref.)
2 tsps.	Baking powder
1 tsp.	Baking soda
½ tsp.	Salt
2 tsps.	Cinnamon
1 tsp.	Nutmeg
1 ½ tsps.	Cardamom
¼ cup (½ stick)	Unsalted butter (Land O'Lakes pref.), melted
¾ cup	Vegetable oil (Wesson pref.)

4 XL	Eggs, room temp.
2 cups	Domino Sugar
2 cups	Pear puree (from 6 or 7 very ripe Anjou, Bartlett, or Comice pears)
½ cup	Pear, diced
2 Tbs.	Crystallized ginger, finely chopped
½ cup, scant	Raw hazelnuts, chopped (optional)

Directions: **Preheat oven to 350 degrees**

1. Grease 3 9-inch pans with Crisco; line bottoms with wax paper. Sift together dry ingredients. In a glass measuring cup, combine melted butter and oil.

2. In a large bowl, vigorously whisk eggs by hand until foamy, adding sugar in a steady stream. Continue whisking until mixture is light in color and well combined.

3. Peel, core, and roughly chop ripe pears (reserving some for dicing). Puree in a food processor (do *not* do this ahead as puree will turn dark). Dice reserved pear to yield ½ cup. Whisk 2 cups of pear puree into egg/sugar mixture, then add in butter/oil.

4. Gently whisk in dry ingredients by large spoonfuls until just combined. Then, with a large rubber spatula, fold in diced pears and ginger (and hazelnuts, if using).

5. **Bake at 350 for 22-23 minutes** until lightly golden, tester comes out clean, and center springs back when lightly touched. Cool in pans 10 minutes on wire racks, then turn layers out onto racks, remove wax paper, and cool for 1 hour. Using plastic wrap, cover tops and tuck around sides after 30 minutes. Frost with Vanilla Cream Cheese Icing, dome side down, allowing for a crumb coat. Chill cake overnight.

Can be made up to two days ahead, chilled, and brought back to room temp. (3-4 hours out) or served slightly chilled.

Can be frozen in an airtight cake carrier, moved to fridge the day before serving.

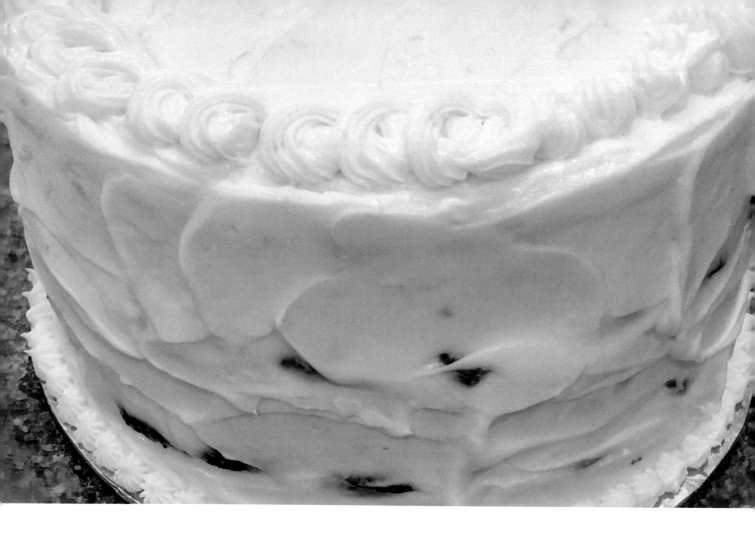

Vanilla & Fresh Strawberry Cake

A very tall, elegant cake....iced with Fresh Lemon Cream Cheese Icing. The combination of the simple cake, fresh berries, and bright icing is outstanding.

Use the large batch recipe of Lemon Cream Cheese Icing for this beauty!

Ingredients:

3 cups	Cake flour (Softasilk or Swans Down)
1 Tbs.	Baking powder
½ tsp.	Salt
1 cup (2 sticks)	Unsalted Butter (Land O'Lakes pref.), room temp.
2 cups	Domino Sugar
5 XL	Eggs, room temp.
1 Tbs.	Mexican vanilla
1 ⅓ cups	Whole buttermilk, shake well before measuring
2 lbs.	Fresh strawberries, washed, hulled, laid to dry, sliced medium thin

Directions: Preheat oven to 350 degrees

1. Grease 3 9-inch pans with Crisco, line bottoms with wax paper, dust sides with cake flour. Sift together dry ingredients; stir vanilla into the buttermilk.

2. Using a standing mixer with paddle attachment, beat butter until smooth, gradually adding sugar in a steady stream. Cream together for 3 minutes on medium-high until light in color and fluffy. Add eggs one at a time on medium, beating well after each. Scrape bowl and mix briefly.

3. Gradually add dry ingredients by large spoonfuls alternately with buttermilk on low, starting and ending with dry ingredients. Scrape bowl and continue mixing just until fully incorporated; mix batter on low for an additional 10 seconds.

4. **Bake at 350 for 22-23 minutes** until tester comes out with moist crumbs attached and center is just set. Do not overbake! Cool in pans 10 minutes on wire racks, then turn layers out onto racks, remove wax paper, and cool for 1 hour. Using plastic wrap, cover tops and tuck around sides after 30 minutes.

5. Place 1st cake layer dome side up on a cake board or very flat serving plate. Add a generous number of berries directly onto layer, then a large dollop of icing, smoothing with a spatula. Repeat with 2nd layer, berries, and icing. Add the final cake layer and use a very little bit of icing around the sides and top for a crumb coat, pushing berries back into place as needed. Chill cake for 1 hour under a cake dome, then proceed with the finish coat of icing. Use additional icing to pipe decoratively around bottom and top edges of cake. Chill cake overnight.

Best made only one day ahead, chilled, and brought back to slight room temp. (2-3 hours out) or served chilled.
Use a serrated knife to cut, if needed. Cannot be frozen.

Amaretto Whipped Cream

Serve alongside my elegant, intensely chocolate, Fallen Angel. Or on top of my Homemade Chocolate Pudding. The Amaretto in this is subtle and delicious - leftovers are great in coffee (or by the spoonful!).

Ingredients:

2 cups	Heavy whipping cream (not organic)
2 Tbs., slightly rounded	Regular sour cream (Breakstone's or similar)
3 ½ Tbs.	Domino Confectioners Sugar
3 ½ Tbs.	Domino (granulated) Sugar
3 Tbs. (generous!)	Disaronno Amaretto
1 tsp.	Mexican vanilla

Directions:

1. Chill a serving bowl or container in the fridge before starting. Chill bowl and whisk attachment of a standing mixer in freezer. Stir together both sugars in a small bowl with a fork.

2. Using the standing mixer on medium-high, whisk together heavy cream and sour cream. Turn mixer to low and add in sugars in a steady stream, then add Amaretto and vanilla. Increase mixer speed to high and beat until thick, fluffy, and *very* stiff peaks form.

3. Scoop whipped cream into the chilled serving bowl or container and place back into the fridge, covered. The Amaretto Whipped Cream must stay chilled until just before serving.

4. When serving with the Fallen Angel, place a small dollop just to the side of each piece.

5. When serving with my Homemade Chocolate Pudding, top the pudding generously with the whipped cream, then decorate with a dusting of cocoa or fine chocolate shavings (from a bar "zested" with a fine grater).

I find that organic heavy cream doesn't whip as well as regular. The sour cream in this recipe stabilizes the whipped cream so that it won't "weep" or become loose. You certainly can change up the type of booze used, but I love the smoothness of the Amaretto, especially up against anything chocolate!

Chocolate Sour Cream Icing

for Devil's Food Layer and Old-Fashioned Vanilla Cakes

This will frost one 9" 3-layer Devil's Food Layer or Old-Fashioned Vanilla Cake. This icing is very smooth and has a depth of chocolate flavor that can't be beat! The Mexican vanilla lends a floral note that's very special.

Ingredients:

1 ¼ cups (2 ½ sticks)	Unsalted butter (Land O' Lakes pref.) cold, cut into pieces
5 oz. (1 ¼ bars)	Ghirardelli's Semi-Sweet Chocolate, chopped
¾ cup + 2 Tbs.	Hershey's Cocoa Powder
1 ½ - 2 Tbs.	Mexican vanilla
4 ⅓ cups, slightly rounded	Domino Confectioners Sugar, sifted
¾ cup + 3 Tbs. (both slightly rounded)	Regular sour cream (Breakstone's or similar)

Directions:

1. Melt butter and chocolate together in a double boiler or a metal bowl set over a pot of 2-inches of simmering water on medium-low heat. When melted, whisk until smooth. Whisk cocoa immediately into warm chocolate and remove from heat to cool slightly.

2. Pour still warm chocolate mixture into a standing mixer bowl. With whisk attachment and mixer on low, gradually add in sifted confectioners sugar by large spoonfuls alternatively with sour cream. Scrape sides and bottom of bowl and beat on medium-high until smooth. Add 1 ½ Tbs. of vanilla, mix and taste, adding more as needed.

3. Chill icing uncovered for 1.5-2 hours until firmed up but spreadable. Always frost the Devil's Food and Old-Fashioned Vanilla Cakes dome side down and do a crumb coat. Chill the cake under a cake dome for 1 hour, then finish with the rest of the icing. Use a piping bag with a small or medium star tip to decorate the bottom and top edges of the cake. This icing typically needs to be re-chilled for 30 minutes while the crumb coat sets up, especially if your kitchen is at all warm.

Cakes made with this icing must be refrigerated.

Icing can be made the day before, left out at room temp. 2-2.5 hours to soften enough to be spreadable.

Chocolate Sour Cream Icing (large batch)

for Devil's Food Sheet Cakes

This will frost one 2-layer 1/4 sheet cake. For a single-layer sheet cake, use the Chocolate Sour Cream Icing recipe for layer cakes.

Ingredients:

1 ¾ cups (3 ½ sticks)	Unsalted butter (Land O' Lakes pref.), cold, cut into pieces
7 oz. (1 ¾ bars)	Ghirardelli's Semi-Sweet Chocolate, chopped
1 cup, slightly rounded	Hershey's Cocoa Powder
2 - 2 ½ Tbs.	Mexican vanilla
6 ⅛ cups, slightly rounded	Domino Confectioners Sugar, sifted
16 oz. (1 container)	Regular sour cream (Breakstone's or similar)

Directions:

1. Melt butter and chocolate together in a double boiler or a metal bowl set over a pot of 2-inches of simmering water on medium-low heat. When melted, whisk until smooth. Whisk cocoa immediately into warm chocolate and remove from heat to cool slightly.

2. Pour still warm chocolate mixture into a standing mixer bowl. With whisk attachment and mixer on low, gradually add in sifted confectioners sugar by large spoonfuls alternatively with sour cream. Scrape sides and bottom of bowl and beat on medium-high until smooth. Add 2 Tbs. of vanilla, mix and taste, adding more as needed.

3. Chill icing uncovered for 2-2.5 hours until firmed up but spreadable. Frost sheet cake dome side up and do a crumb coat; chill cake for 1 hour inside a large bakery box, then finish with the rest of the icing. Use a piping bag with a medium or large star tip to decorate the bottom and top edges of the cake.

(Note: You'll have to be very careful when flipping each sheet cake out of its pan to form 2-layers. And you'll need a large rectangular foil-wrapped cake board and large wire racks to help you).

Cakes made with this icing must be refrigerated.

Icing can be made the day before, left out at room temp. 2.5-3 hours to soften enough to be spreadable.

Photo credit: Jakub's Food Photography on Creative Market

Luscious Coconut Icing

for Luscious Coconut and Mounds Cakes

This will frost one 9" 3-layer Luscious Coconut or Mounds Cake (with icing left over when using on the Mounds).

Ingredients:

12 oz.	Regular cream cheese (Philadelphia brand pref.), softened
½ cup (1 stick)	Unsalted butter (Land O'Lakes pref.) very soft
5 cups, slightly rounded	Domino Confectioners Sugar, sifted
¼ cup	Regular coconut milk (Thai Kitchen Organic or similar)
¾ tsp.	Mexican vanilla
2 - 3 tsps.	Coconut extract
1 14-oz. bag	Baker's Angel Flake Sweetened Coconut

Directions:

1. Using a standing mixer with paddle attachment, cream butter and cream cheese together on medium-high until fluffy and well combined.

2. Gradually add in half the sifted confectioners sugar by large spoonfuls with mixer on low; blend in all of the coconut milk, then slowly add the rest of the sugar. Scrape bowl and continue to beat until smooth. Add vanilla and 2 tsps. of the coconut extract, mix and taste the icing, and add more of the coconut extract as needed.

3. Chill icing for 1-1.5 hours covered, until set and ready to use. The icing should be slightly firm but spreadable. The Luscious Coconut Cake does not require a crumb coat, but it does help ensure that the icing doesn't squeeze out between the layers. Always frost the Coconut Cake dome side down. Gently press generous amounts of coconut onto each layer as you ice it, then onto the sides and top of the cake as you complete the (finish layer of) icing. For the Mounds Cake, always frost it dome side up, and be generous with the coconut between the layers and on top. The sides will get a fabulous chocolate ganache!

Note: Laying wax paper underneath the cake turntable will help you catch any wayward coconut so that you can use all of it!

Cakes made with this icing must be refrigerated.

Icing can be made the day before, left out at room temp. 2-2.5 hours to soften enough to be spreadable.

Coconut-Pecan Icing

for German Chocolate Cakes

This will just frost one 9" 3-layer German Chocolate Cake. So go easy between the layers to ensure you'll have enough icing for the sides and top!

Plan ahead as icing is best made the day before.

Ingredients:

1 12-oz. can	Evaporated milk (PET or similar)
1 ½ cups, slightly rounded	Domino Sugar
¾ cup (1 ½ sticks)	Unsalted butter (Land O'Lakes pref.), cold, cut into pieces
4 XL	Egg yolks, room temp., slightly beaten
1 ½ tsps.	Mexican vanilla
7 oz.	Baker's Angel Flake Sweetened Coconut
1 ½ cups, slightly rounded	Pecans* (measure first, then chop)

Directions:

1. Have all ingredients prepped and measured before starting. Chop whole pecans fairly fine by pulsing in a food processor (some smallish pieces are ok).

2. Pour evaporated milk into a heavy-bottomed pot and, off heat, whisk in granulated sugar and lightly beaten eggs yolks; add cold butter.

3. On medium heat, cook the icing for 12-15 minutes. Use a large rubber spatula to constantly stir until thickened and an instant-read thermometer reaches 165 degrees. Do not allow icing to boil. Add vanilla for the last 1 minute of cooking.

4. Off heat, immediately stir in coconut and pecans. Pour icing into a large bowl and cool on the counter, uncovered, for at least 1 hour. Cover tightly with plastic wrap and chill overnight before using. Always frost the German Chocolate Cake dome side down (a crumb coat is not possible). Decorate the top edge of cake with whole candied pecans.

Candied pecans: Pick out nice looking whole pecans and sauté them in a little butter on low, adding granulated sugar to coat. After nuts have lightly browned, stir in a dash of vanilla at the end. Take care not to over-brown nuts as they burn easily! Immediately remove nuts to a plate and chill uncovered before using. (Can be made one day ahead if kept chilled, in a single layer, inside of an airtight container).

* When using whole nuts, always place nuts on a large plate and look for any partial shells or discoloration and discard those nuts before chopping.

Cakes made with this icing must be refrigerated.

Lemon Cream Cheese Icing

for Lemon & Fresh Blueberry Cakes

This icing is creamy, not overly sweet, with layers of lemon taste! This will frost one 9" 3-layer Lemon & Fresh Blueberry Cake.

Ingredients:

16 oz.	Regular cream cheese (Philadelphia brand pref.), softened
¾ cup (1 ½ sticks)	Unsalted butter (Land O'Lakes pref.), very soft
4 ½ cups, slightly rounded	Domino Confectioners Sugar, sifted
1 Large	Lemon for zesting
1 tsp.	Mexican vanilla
1 ¼ tsps.	Lemon extract
¼ tsp.	Lemon oil

Directions:

1. Using a standing mixer with paddle attachment, cream butter and cream cheese together on medium-high until somewhat combined. Add fresh zest and continue beating to release the oils, until mixture is fluffy and well blended.

2. Gradually add in sifted confectioners sugar by large spoonfuls with mixer on low; scrape bowl and continue to mix until smooth. Add extracts, mix and taste the icing, and add a tiny bit more of the lemon extract as needed.

3. Chill icing for 1-1.5 hours covered, until just set and ready to use. The icing should be slightly firm but spreadable. Always frost the Lemon & Fresh Blueberry Cake dome side up, choosing the layer with the fewest berries as your bottom layer. Do a crumb coat and chill the cake under a cake dome for 1 hour, then finish with the rest of the icing. Use a piping bag with a small or medium star tip to decorate the bottom and top edges of the cake.

Cakes made with this icing must be refrigerated.

Icing can be made the day before, left out at room temp. 2-2.5 hours to soften enough to be spreadable.

Lemon Cream Cheese Icing (large batch)

for Vanilla & Fresh Strawberry Cakes

This will frost one 9" 3-layer Vanilla & Fresh Strawberry Cake. This is a larger batch of icing, as the vanilla layers and almost 2 lbs. of fresh strawberries result in a very tall cake!

Ingredients:

19 oz.	Regular cream cheese (Philadelphia brand pref.), softened
⅞ cup (1 ¾ sticks)	Unsalted butter (Land O'Lakes pref.), very soft
5 ⅓ cups, slightly rounded	Domino Confectioners Sugar, sifted
1 ½ Large	Lemons for zesting
1 ¼ tsps.	Mexican vanilla
1 ½ tsps.	Lemon extract
⅓ tsp.	Lemon oil

Directions:

1. Using a standing mixer with paddle attachment, cream butter and cream cheese together on medium-high until somewhat combined. Add fresh zest and continue beating to release the oils, until mixture is fluffy and well blended.

2. Gradually add in sifted confectioners sugar by large spoonfuls with mixer on low; scrape bowl and continue to mix until smooth. Add extracts, mix and taste the icing, and add a tiny bit more of the lemon extract as needed.

3. Chill icing for 1.5-2 hours covered, until just set and ready to use. The icing should be slightly firm but spreadable. Always frost the Vanilla & Fresh Strawberry Cake dome side up. Add lots of fresh berries on the first layer, then some of the lemon icing. Repeat with the next layer, berries, then icing. Finish with the top layer and do a crumb coat. You'll need to push the berries back into position as you do this first coat. Chill the cake under a dome for 1 hour, then finish with the rest of the icing. Use a piping bag with a small or medium star tip to decorate the bottom and top edges of the cake.

Note: the fresh berries will bleed through the icing, but this is to be expected and should be celebrated! Who doesn't love to see the evidence of fresh juicy berries?

Cakes made with this icing must be refrigerated.

Icing can be made the day before, left out at room temp. 2.5-3 hours to soften enough to be spreadable.

Photo credit: Tara Winstead on Pexels

Photo credit: MG_Production on Creative Market

Fresh Orange Cream Cheese Icing

for Island Carrot Cakes

This will frost one 9" 3-layer Island Carrot Cake. The fresh orange zest gives this icing such a bright taste!

Ingredients:

16 oz.	Regular cream cheese (Philadelphia brand pref.), softened
¾ cup (1 ½ sticks)	Unsalted butter (Land O'Lakes pref.), very soft
4 ½ cups, slightly rounded	Domino Confectioners Sugar, sifted
1 Large	Orange for zesting
1 tsp.	Mexican vanilla
1 ¼ tsps.	Orange extract

Directions:

1. Using a standing mixer with paddle attachment, cream butter and cream cheese together on medium-high until somewhat combined. Add fresh zest and continue beating to release the oils, until mixture is fluffy and well blended.

2. Gradually add in sifted confectioners sugar by large spoonfuls with mixer on low; scrape bowl and continue mixing until smooth. Add extracts, mix and taste the icing, and add a tiny bit more of the orange extract as needed.

3. Chill icing for 1-1.5 hours covered, until just set and ready to use. The icing should be slightly firm but spreadable. Always frost the Island Carrot Cake dome side down and do a crumb coat. Chill the cake under a cake dome for 1 hour, then finish with the rest of the icing. Use a piping bag with a small or medium star tip to decorate the bottom and top edges of the cake; immediately sprinkle icing with chilled candied walnuts.

Candied walnuts: Roughly chop whole walnuts (or buy as chopped); sauté nuts in little butter on low, then add granulated sugar to coat. Stir nuts while browning – be sure not to overcook, as they can burn easily! Finish with a dash of vanilla and cinnamon. Immediately scoop nuts onto a plate and chill (uncovered) until they have hardened and sugar has crystalized. Can be made two days before, stored in the fridge in an airtight container.

Cakes made with this icing must be refrigerated.

Icing can be made the day before, left out at room temp. 2-2.5 hours to soften enough to be spreadable.

Vanilla Cream Cheese Icing

for Pumpkin Spice and Fresh Pear Cakes

This will frost one 9" 3-layer Pumpkin Spice or Fresh Pear Cake. Perfect for any cake that calls for a classic cream cheese icing!

Ingredients:

16 oz.	Regular cream cheese (Philadelphia brand pref.), softened
¾ cups (1 ½ sticks)	Unsalted butter (Land O'Lakes pref.), very soft
4 ½ cups, slightly rounded	Domino Confectioners Sugar, sifted
1 ½ Tbs.	Mexican vanilla

Directions:

1. Using a standing mixer with paddle attachment, cream butter and cream cheese together on medium-high until fluffy and well combined.

2. Gradually add in sifted confectioners sugar by large spoonfuls with mixer on low; scrape bowl and continue to mix until smooth. Add vanilla, mix and taste the icing, and add a bit more as needed.

3. Chill icing for 1-1.5 hours covered, until just set and ready to use. The icing should be slightly firm but spreadable. Always frost the Pumpkin Spice and Fresh Pear Cakes dome side down and do a crumb coat. Chill the cake under a cake dome for 1 hour, then finish with the rest of the icing. Use a piping bag with a small or medium star tip to decorate the bottom and top edges of the cake.

Cakes made with this icing must be refrigerated.

Icing can be made the day before, left out at room temp. 2-2.5 hours to soften enough to be spreadable.

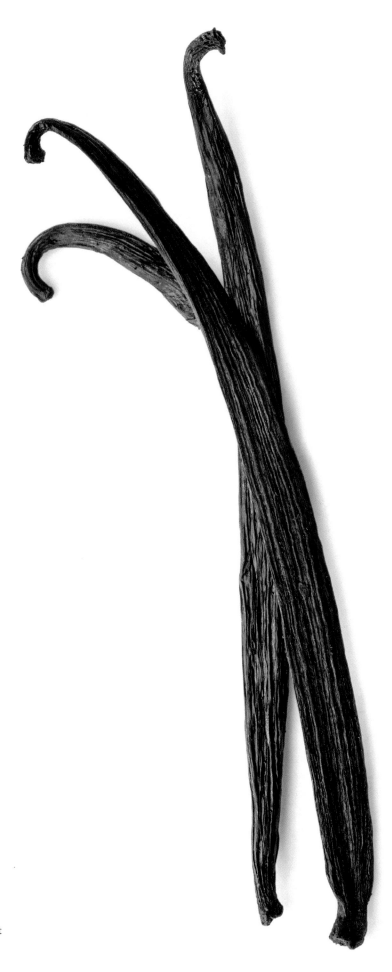

Photo credit: Volff on Creative Market

COOKIES

Giant Chocolate Chip Cookies

Chocolate Chunk Cookies

Chocolate Frangelico Crinkles

Coconut Macaroons

Old-Fashioned Ginger Molasses Cookies

Greek Wedding Cookies

Homemade Ice Cream Sandwiches

Italian Lemon Drops

Lemon Butter Twists

Mint Butter Twists

Peanut Butter Chocolate Chip Cookies

Peanut Butter Kisses

Pignoli (Pine Nut) Cookies

Mary Jane's Pumpkin Cookies

Soft Sugar Cookies

Steel-Cut Oatmeal Cookies with White Chocolate and Cherries

Triple Trouble Chocolate Cookies

BAR COOKIES

Break My Heart Brownies

Brown Butter Blondies

Amaretto Cheesecake Brownie Bites

Mint Cheesecake Brownie Bites

Vanilla Cheesecake Brownie Bites

Mary Lee's Famous M&M Bars

Snickerdoodle Bars

Cookie & Bar Cookie Tips & Tricks

Measuring and Mixing

Two key tricks to successful cookie baking (all baking actually!) have to do with measuring your flour and mixing in your dry ingredients, e.g., flour, baking powder, baking soda, salt, ground spices.

The most accurate way to measure flour for any baking recipe is to use a large serving spoon or flour-scoop to gently fill your dry measuring cup; use a straight-edged knife or icing spatula to level that off. Do this over wax paper to avoid a mess and to avoid wasting flour. Never use your measuring cup to scoop into your flour, as this will pack it into the cup, yielding much more than you need. I've experimented with this - using a food scale to weigh results - and the difference is amazing. That incidental increase in flour volume can be the difference between a delicate and moist cookie versus a heavy and dry one.

Always sift together your dry ingredients (remember, dry ingredients do *not* include your sugar), then use a large spoon to gradually add them into the cookie dough with your mixer on low or fold them in by hand. Overbeating at this stage will build up the gluten in your flour, resulting in a tough cookie or overly dense bar.

Temperature and Time

As with batches of cupcakes, it is important to maintain your oven temperature when baking cookies. Always wait to slide in your second and third sheet pans until the oven has gone back to the designated temperature. This will ensure an even bake for each pan.

Most published cookie and bar cookie recipes call for too long a bake time, so always bake for the *least* amount of time indicated and add more (by 30 seconds for cookies and one minute for bars) until you think they are perfect.

Cooling

So many recipes call for you to cool cookies on racks - just don't! As I like to tell anyone who'll listen: "Air is not a cookie's friend". Always bake your cookies on parchment paper, then use that to slide them onto the counter to cool completely. Write down when each pan comes out of the oven so that you'll know when to pack the cookies into airtight containers. Most cookies are ready to be packed up after 45 minutes, up to one hour. They should not sit out longer than that. Don't unwrap your cookie platters until right before serving. Sounds simple, but I've seen many a well-meaning host/hostess dry cookies out by unwrapping them too early.

Giant Chocolate Chip Cookies

Always a favorite with customers, with my youngest son Nick, and at the café at Bards Alley! Their huge size gives them that "wow" factor, and their crisp edge, soft center makes them the perfect cookie!

These cookies are best served on the first or second day.

Ingredients:

2 ¼ cups	All-purpose flour (Gold Medal pref.)
½ tsp.	Baking powder
½ tsp.	Baking soda
1 tsp.	Salt
½ cup (1 stick)	Unsalted butter (Land O'Lakes pref.), room temp.
½ cup, slightly rounded	Crisco Vegetable Shortening, room temp.
¾ cup, level	Domino Sugar
¾ cup, packed, slightly rounded	Domino Light Brown Sugar
2 XL	Eggs, room temp.
1 ½ tsps.	Mexican vanilla
1 Tbs., rounded	Regular sour cream (Breakstone's or similar)
1 lb.	Nestlé Semi-Sweet Chocolate chips

Directions: **Preheat oven to 350 degrees**

1. Sift together dry ingredients. Using a standing mixer with paddle attachment, beat butter and Crisco together on medium-high until smooth. Add both sugars together and cream mixture until light and fluffy.

2. Add eggs one at a time on medium, beating well after each. Blend in sour cream and vanilla, scrape bowl, and mix again briefly.

3. Gradually add in dry ingredients by large spoonfuls on low; scrape sides and bottom of bowl and continue mixing just until fully incorporated. Stir in chocolate chips on low.

4. Scoop dough using a ¼ cup dry measuring cup (rounded shape!). Only fill level to the top. Using a small rubber spatula, scoop out dough onto parchment-lined cookie sheets, 5 to a pan (two on each end, one in the middle). Flatten each mound slightly with dampened fingertips.

5. **Bake at 350 for 13-14 minutes** until edges are just golden (centers should still look pale). Allow cookies to cool on pans for 3 minutes, then slide the parchment onto counter to cool cookies completely.

Makes 15 giant cookies. Can be stored for one or two days at room temp. in airtight containers.

To freeze: chill cookies, then place them into individual zip-lock bags and freeze inside large containers.

Chocolate Chunk Cookies

These cookies are studded with lots of large chocolate chunks (plus some minis)! These were always part of my Valentine's Day Specials as my "Bags of Love".

Plan ahead as dough must chill overnight (can be made up to two days before).

Ingredients:

2 cups	All-purpose flour (Gold Medal pref.)
½ cup	Cake flour (Softasilk or Swans Down)
½ tsp.	Baking powder
½ tsp.	Baking soda
1 tsp.	Salt
½ cup (1 stick)	Unsalted butter (Land O'Lakes pref.), room temp.
½ cup, slightly rounded	Crisco Vegetable Shortening, room temp.
¾ cup level	Domino Sugar
¾ cup, packed, slightly rounded	Domino Light Brown Sugar
2 XL	Eggs, room temp.
1 ½ tsps.	Mexican vanilla
1 Tbs., rounded	Regular sour cream (Breakstone's or similar)
15 oz.	Nestlé Semi-Sweet Chocolate Chunks
4 oz.	Ghirardelli Semi-Sweet Mini Chips

Directions: **Preheat oven to 350 degrees**

1. Sift together dry ingredients. Using a standing mixer with paddle attachment, beat butter and Crisco together on medium-high until smooth. Add both sugars together and cream mixture until light and fluffy.

2. Add eggs one at a time on medium, beating well after each. Blend in sour cream and vanilla, scrape bowl, and mix again briefly.

3. Gradually add in dry ingredients by large spoonfuls on low; scrape sides and bottom of bowl and continue mixing just until fully incorporated. Stir in chocolate chunks and mini chips on low. Chill dough overnight.

4. Scoop dough using a rounded household teaspoon and roll quickly into balls. Place balls onto parchment-lined cookie sheets, 9 to a pan.

5. **Bake at 350 for 11.5-12 minutes** until edges are golden. Allow cookies to cool on pans for 2 minutes, then slide the parchment onto counter to cool cookies completely.

Makes 30-35 cookies. Can be stored for several days at room temp. (or frozen) in airtight containers.

Photo by Rich Kessler Photography

Chocolate Frangelico Crinkles

My recipe was included in The Washington Post's Annual Holiday Cookie Issue in December 2011 (along with my M&M Bar recipe!). These are very adult cookies that always sold well at Christmastime. Expensive to make, but very special when you do.

Plan ahead as dough must chill overnight.

Ingredients:

1 ¼ cups	All-purpose flour (Gold Medal pref.)
1 Tbs.	Baking powder
½ tsp.	Salt
12 oz. (3 bars)	Ghirardelli Semi-Sweet Chocolate, chopped
6 Tbs. (¾ stick)	Unsalted butter (Land O'Lakes pref.), cold, cut into pieces
2 XL	Eggs, room temp.
½ cup + 3 Tbs.	Domino Sugar
6 Tbs.	Frangelico hazelnut liqueur
¼ cup	Heavy whipping cream
1 Tbs.	Mexican vanilla
1 cup	Domino Confectioners Sugar, sifted onto plate

Directions: **Preheat oven to 350 degrees**

1. Sift together dry ingredients. Melt chocolate with butter in a double boiler over medium-low heat or set a metal bowl over a pot of 2-inches of simmering water; when melted, whisk until smooth. Remove from heat to cool slightly.

2. In a large bowl, whisk eggs and sugar together vigorously by hand until very light in color and starting to thicken. Add in chocolate mixture, Frangelico, cream, and vanilla, whisking well after each. Gently fold in dry ingredients with a large rubber spatula. Chill dough overnight.

3. Scoop dough using a slightly rounded household Tablespoon, then roll between (slightly dampened) palms. Next, roll each ball in powdered sugar to coat thoroughly. Place 2-inches apart on parchment-lined cookie sheets, 12 to a pan.

4. **Bake at 350 for 12-13 minutes** until puffed, cracked, but still soft in the center. Allow cookies to cool on pans for 3 minutes, then slide the parchment onto counter to cool cookies completely.

Makes approx. 30 cookies. Can be stored for several days at room temp. in airtight containers. These freeze really well. (Note: a mini version can be made using a household teaspoon instead and baking at 350 for 10-11 minutes for a yield of approx. 50 cookies).

Coconut Macaroons

Naturally Gluten-Free! Mine are soft and so delicious! These were sold at Bards Alley Bookstore & Café as Almond Joy Macaroons and were always very popular.

Plan ahead as macaroons should chill overnight before being glazed.

Ingredients:

4 XL	Egg whites, room temp.
½ cup, rounded	Domino Sugar
¼ + ⅛ tsps.	Almond extract (Nielsen-Massey pref.)
1 tsp.	Mexican vanilla
Pinch	Salt
1 14-oz. bag	Baker's Angel Flake Sweetened Coconut
1 2-oz. bag	Sliced raw almonds
4 oz.	Nestlé Semi-Sweet Chocolate chips
3 Tbs.	Whole milk
Dash	Vanilla
Dash	Light corn syrup

Directions:

1. Chill bowl and whisk attachment of a standing mixer in freezer. In the well-chilled bowl, beat the eggs whites, sugar, extracts, and salt together on medium-high until glossy white and thick (3 full minutes).

2. Gently fold coconut in by hand with a large rubber spatula (batter will be very moist). Then drop by household Tablespoons (using your fingers to form cookies into tall, rounded stacks) onto parchment-lined cookie sheets, 12 to a pan.

3. **Bake at 325 for 18-20 minutes** until set and tops are slightly golden brown. Allow cookies to cool on pans for 5 minutes, then slide the parchment onto counter to cool cookies completely. Chill cookies overnight before glazing.

Chocolate glaze:

Melt chocolate with milk in a double boiler over medium-low heat or set a metal bowl over a pot of 2-inches of simmering water; when melted, whisk until smooth, then whisk in vanilla and corn syrup. Dip the top of each cold macaroon into warm glaze and place a single almond slice on each while glaze is still wet. Place finished cookies on wax paper lined baking pans and return to fridge *uncovered* to chill thoroughly. Move to airtight containers only when glaze has hardened, storing in a single layer. Macaroons are best served cold.

Makes approx. 24 cookies (recipe can be doubled). Can be stored for several days, chilled, in airtight containers.

Can be frozen until ready to glaze.

Old-Fashioned Ginger Molasses Cookies

These were always part of my Cookie Carousels during the holidays and had a very loyal following! Mine are large, soft cookies with a complex spiciness.

Plan ahead as dough must chill overnight.

Cookies are best the day after baking.

Ingredients:

4 cups	All-purpose flour (Gold Medal pref.)
1 cup	Domino Sugar
2 tsps.	Baking soda
2 tsps., slightly rounded	Ginger
1 tsp., slightly rounded	Nutmeg
1 tsp., slightly rounded	Cinnamon

1 tsp., slightly rounded	Cloves
½ tsp.	Salt
1 cup	Grandma's Original Molasses (not Robust)
½ cup, slightly rounded	Crisco Vegetable Shortening
1 XL	Egg, room temp., slightly beaten
½ cup	Boiling water (boil first, then measure)
Extra	Granulated sugar for rolling

Directions: Preheat oven to 400 degrees

1. Measure molasses in a lightly oiled glass measuring cup. Sift together dry ingredients directly into a very large bowl, then cut in molasses, Crisco, and egg with a hand-held pastry blender until roughly combined.

2. Transfer dough to a standing mixer bowl, and with paddle attachment, mix very briefly on medium. Turning mixer to low, add the boiling water in a steady stream and beat *just* until dough is fully blended. Scrape bowl and mix briefly. Chill dough overnight.

3. Scoop dough using a household Tablespoon, then roll between (slightly dampened) palms into balls. The dough must remain cold while forming balls, so you'll need to work quickly. Next, roll each ball into extra sugar to coat evenly, doing a few cookies at a time. Place balls 2-inches apart on parchment-lined cookie sheets, 9 to a pan.

4. **Bake at 400 for 10-10.5 minutes** until cookies are puffed, cracked, but still soft in the center. Allow cookies to cool on pans for 2 minutes, then slide the parchment onto counter to cool cookies completely.

Makes approx. 35 large cookies. Best if made one day ahead and allowed to soften in airtight containers at room temp. These will stay fresh for several days, and they freeze really well.

Greek Wedding Cookies

Adapted from a recipe of one of my mom's closest friends, Mrs. Efdemis, who was from Greece. I remember eating these as a child and loving them. Mine are nicely spiced and melt-in-your-mouth delicious.

Plan ahead as these need to "age" two to three days before serving.

Ingredients:

½ cup	Domino Confectioners Sugar, sifted
1 cup (2 sticks)	Unsalted butter (Land O'Lakes pref.), very soft
2 ¼ cups + 2 Tbs.	All-purpose flour (Gold Medal pref.), sifted
½ cup	Finely chopped walnuts, measure after chopping (so start with more)
1 tsp.	Mexican vanilla
Plateful	Confectioners sugar, sifted
Several dashes	Cloves
Several dashes	Allspice
Dash	Cinnamon

Directions:

1. In a food processor with metal blade insert, *very* finely chop whole walnuts, then measure out ½ cup. Combine sifted confectioners sugar with 2 cups of the sifted flour in a standing mixer bowl. Using the paddle attachment on low, stir until well blended, add nuts and mix briefly; add all of the butter at once and vanilla. Continue to mix on low until just combined. Scrape bowl and mix very briefly.

2. Turn dough out into a large bowl or onto countertop lined with wax paper and add in remaining flour; knead gently with fingertips until thoroughly combined.

3. Pinch off dough and roll into 1.5-inch balls, then form into crescent shapes by rolling in between your palms (or you can keep cookies round). Place onto parchment-lined cookie sheets, 15 to a pan.

4. **Bake at 325 for 13-13.5 minutes** until barely golden on the bottom and just set. Allow cookies to cool on pans for 2 minutes, then slide the parchment onto counter to cool cookies slightly.

5. While cookies are baking, combine a plateful of sifted confectioners sugar and spices, taste and adjust: allspice and cloves should be the dominant flavors (not cinnamon). Carefully place warm cookies on top of the spiced sugar and cover each cookie entirely with the mixture. It is best to work with only a few cookies at a time, and you'll need to work quickly for the sugar to adhere properly. Allow cookies to cool completely on wax paper.

Makes 26-30 cookies. Store at room temp. two to three days before serving for best taste and texture.

Can be frozen in airtight containers (I save some leftover spiced sugar to re-coat cookies once thawed).

Homemade Ice Cream Sandwiches

My Triple Trouble Chocolate Cookies with premium ice cream sandwiched in between. These are playful make-ahead treats, perfect for summer parties!

Plan ahead as dough must chill overnight before baking the cookies.

You'll need another day to fill and freeze the ice cream sandwiches.

Ingredients:

2 oz.	Baker's Unsweetened Chocolate, chopped
8 oz.	Nestlé Semi-Sweet Chocolate chips
6 Tbs. (¾ stick)	Unsalted butter (Land O'Lakes pref.), cold, cut into pieces
3 Tbs.	Hershey's Cocoa Powder
1 ½ tsps.	Mexican vanilla
1 cup	All-purpose flour (Gold Medal pref.)
1 tsp.	Baking powder
¾ tsp.	Salt

3 XL	Eggs, room temp.
1 cup, slightly rounded	Domino Sugar
½ cup	Nestlé Semi-Sweet Chocolate chips
½ cup	Nestlé White Chocolate chips
1 Large container (or several small ones)	Premium ice cream (Haagen Dazs or similar), any flavor that works well with chocolate (coffee, cherry, mint choc., etc.)

Directions: **Preheat oven to 350 degrees**

1. Melt both chocolates with butter in a double boiler over medium-low heat or set a metal bowl over a pot of 2-inches of simmering water; when melted, whisk until smooth. Immediately whisk in cocoa to "melt" off heat. Cool slightly, then add vanilla.

2. Sift together dry ingredients. Combine dark and white chips in a small bowl.

3. Using a standing mixer with whisk attachment, beat eggs and add sugar in a steady stream, mixing on medium-high until frothy and starting to thicken. Switching to paddle attachment, blend in chocolate mixture on low, scrape bowl, and mix well.

4. Gradually add in dry ingredients by large spoonfuls on low until just combined (do not overbeat). Stir in both chips. Chill dough overnight.

5. Scoop dough using a slightly heaping household teaspoon, then roll between (slightly dampened) palms into balls. Place balls 2-inches apart on parchment-lined cookie sheets, 12 to a pan.

6. **Bake at 350 for 11-12 minutes** until cookies are puffed, set, but still soft in the center. Allow cookies to cool on pans for 2 minutes, then slide the parchment onto counter to cool cookies completely. Chill cookies overnight before filling.

7. For the ice cream sandwiches, allow your ice cream to soften a bit. Carefully place one small scoop between two cold cookies, squeeze gently, then use a small metal spatula to clean up the edges. If you prefer, you can skip the clean-up and roll the edges in sprinkles or mini chocolate chips instead!

8. Place ice cream sandwiches on a wax paper lined baking sheet pan and "flash freeze" uncovered for 1 hour. Then wrap each individually in plastic and place inside airtight containers. Sandwiches can be enjoyed right from the freezer!

Makes approx. 14 sandwiches. Can be stored in the freezer for up to two weeks until ready to serve.

Italian Lemon Drops

Soft iced cookies with a bright lemon flavor....these can be decorated for any occasion! My Aunt Jo Hessney of Palmyra, New York, used to make something very similar, and I dearly loved hers.

Ingredients:

2 ½ cups	All-purpose flour (Gold Medal pref.)
½ cup	Cornstarch
½ tsp.	Salt
1 cup (2 sticks)	Unsalted butter (Land O'Lakes pref.), very soft
1 ¼ cups, rounded	Domino Confectioners Sugar, sifted
1 ½ Large	Lemons for zesting

4 Tbs.	Fresh lemon juice
½ tsp.	Mexican vanilla
1 cup, rounded	Confectioners sugar, sifted
2 Tbs.	Lemon juice
½ tsp.	Lemon oil
½ tsp.	Vanilla

Directions:

Cookies: **Preheat oven to 350 degrees**

1. Sift together dry ingredients. Using a standing mixer with paddle attachment, cream butter and sifted confectioners sugar on medium-high until fluffy and smooth. Add lemon zest and beat well to release the oils. Slowly add lemon juice and vanilla.

2. Gradually mix in dry ingredients by large spoonfuls on low, scrape bowl, and mix until just combined. The dough must be chilled for at least 1-2 hours (or overnight).

3. Scoop dough using a household teaspoon (do not overfill) and roll into balls. (If dough chilled overnight, leave out for 1 hour to soften slightly). Place balls on parchment-lined baking sheets, 12 to a pan.

4. **Bake at 350 for 10.5-11 minutes** until edges are slightly golden and centers are set. Allow cookies to cool on pans for 2 minutes, then slide the parchment onto counter to cool cookies completely.

Icing:

In a medium bowl, whisk 1 cup of sifted confectioners sugar with lemon juice, lemon oil, and vanilla by hand until smooth. Dip the top of each cookie into icing, allowing it to drip down slightly. Place cookies on wax paper and if using decorations, sprinkle those on top immediately while icing is still wet, decorating only a few cookies at a time.

Makes approx. 28 cookies. Can be stored for several days at room temp. in airtight containers.

Can be frozen before being iced.

Lemon Butter Twists

A snappy lemon version of my popular Mint Butter Twists. These are so elegant and melt-in-your-mouth delicious! The recipe calls for both lemon oil and lemon extract, and that's where the magic happens!

Ingredients:

4 cups	All-purpose flour (Gold Medal pref.)
Pinch	Salt
1 lb. (4 sticks)	Unsalted butter (Land O'Lakes pref.), very soft
4 tsps.	Mexican vanilla
1 ⅛ tsps.	Lemon oil
1 cup + 2 Tbs., slightly rounded	Domino Confectioners Sugar, sifted
1 cup	Confectioners sugar, sifted
1 Tbs. + 1 tsp.	Whole milk
1 Tbs.	Unsalted butter, very soft
1 tsp., scant	Lemon extract
1 tsp.	Vanilla

Directions:

Cookies: **Preheat oven to 350 degrees**

1. Sift together flour and salt. Using a standing mixer with paddle attachment, beat very soft butter, vanilla, and lemon oil on medium-high until fluffy. Add in sifted confectioners sugar with mixer on low; increase speed to medium and cream sugar and butter mixture until smooth and well blended.

2. Turning mixer back to low, gradually add in dry ingredients by large spoonfuls. Scrape bowl and mix briefly just until thoroughly combined.

3. Place dough inside a large pastry bag and pipe onto parchment-lined cookie sheets using a large star tip (I use #864, the "French Star") to make figure 8's or any shape you'd like, 20 to a pan.

4. **Bake at 350 for 8.5-9 minutes** until bottoms are barely golden and cookies are set. Allow cookies to cool on pans for 2 minutes, then slide the parchment onto counter to cool cookies completely. Cookies may be iced the same day as they are baked or iced the following day.

Lemon Icing:

Whisk 1 cup of sifted confectioners sugar, milk, very soft butter, and extracts vigorously by hand until smooth. Pipe icing decoratively over half of each cookie. You can add edible beads or sparkling sugar, but you must do so immediately while the icing is still wet, decorating only a few cookies at a time. I love to press gold nonpareils onto the icing of these cookies.......so pretty!

Makes 60-75 cookies, depending on how you pipe them. Best made one day ahead and stored in the fridge until ready to ice. Decorated cookies can be stored chilled for several days (in a single layer) in airtight containers. Allow cookies to come to room temp. before serving for best taste and texture.

Can be frozen before icing and decorating.

Mint Butter Twists

These are such elegant cookies. Very light and delicate - dipped in mint-scented dark chocolate. They always sold well during the holidays!

Plan ahead as these are best dipped two days before serving.

Ingredients:

4 cups	All-purpose flour (Gold Medal pref.)
Pinch	Salt
1 lb. (4 sticks)	Unsalted butter (Land O'Lakes pref.), very soft
4 tsps.	Mexican vanilla
1 tsp.	Peppermint extract
¼ tsp.	Mint extract
1 cup + 2 Tbs., slightly rounded	Domino Confectioners Sugar, sifted
6 oz.	Nestlé Semi-Sweet Chocolate chips
5 tsps.	Whole milk
2 Tbs.	Unsalted butter, cold

¼ tsp., scant	Peppermint extract
⅛ tsp.	Mint extract
3 tsps.	Crème de Menthe White Liqueur *(optional....use more peppermint or mint extract if not using)*
½ tsp.	Light corn syrup

Directions:

Cookies: **Preheat oven to 350 degrees**

1. Sift together flour and salt. Using a standing mixer with paddle attachment, beat very soft butter, vanilla, and mint extracts on medium-high until fluffy. Add in sifted confectioners sugar with mixer on low; increase speed to medium and cream sugar and butter mixture until well blended.

2. Turning mixer back to low, gradually add in dry ingredients by large spoonfuls. Scrape bowl and mix briefly just until thoroughly combined.

3. Place dough inside a pastry bag and pipe onto parchment-lined cookie sheets using a large star tip (I use #864, the "French Star") to make figure 8's or any shape you'd like, 20 to a pan.

4. **Bake at 350 for 8.5-9 minutes** until bottoms are barely golden and cookies are set. Allow cookies to cool on pans for 2 minutes, then slide the parchment onto counter to cool cookies completely. Store airtight and chill overnight before dipping in glaze.

Chocolate Glaze:

1. Melt chocolate with milk in a double boiler over medium-low heat or set a metal bowl over a pot of 2-inches of simmering water. When melted, whisk until smooth, then add butter, extracts, corn syrup, and liqueur (if using), whisking well after each. Add a tiny bit more milk if the glaze seems too thick. Use the warm glaze immediately.

2. Tip the bowl with glaze on its side and dip half of each cold cookie into the warm glaze. Place cookies on wax paper lined cookie sheets. Chill in fridge for several hours *uncovered* until glaze has hardened. Carefully peel cookies off of the wax paper and store them in a single layer in airtight containers. Keep chilled until ready to serve.

*If you are using decorations (edible beads, sparkling sugar, specialty shapes), you must press or sprinkle these immediately onto each cookie while glaze is still wet. You'll need to work quickly, so only decorate a few cookies at a time.

Makes 60-75 cookies, depending on how you pipe them. Decorated cookies will hold for several days in the fridge, stored in a single layer in airtight containers or carefully wrapped cookie sheets. Can be frozen before glazing and decorating. (Note: The chocolate on these won't hold up in any kind of heat).

Peanut Butter Chocolate Chip Cookies

A new family recipe as of 2020....best of a classic combo, loaded with chocolate! The dough can be made ahead, frozen, thawed, and then baked. So easy!

Ingredients:

2 ½ cups	All-purpose flour (Gold Medal pref.)
1 tsp.	Baking soda
½ tsp.	Salt
½ cup (1 stick)	Unsalted butter (Land O'Lakes pref.), room temp.
¼ cup, slightly rounded	Crisco Vegetable Shortening, room temp.
1 cup, slightly rounded	Skippy Regular Creamy Peanut Butter
1 cup, level	Domino Sugar
1 cup, packed, slightly rounded	Domino Light Brown Sugar
2 XL	Eggs, room temp.
2 tsps.	Mexican vanilla
8 oz.	Nestlé Semi-Sweet Chocolate Chunks
6 oz.	Nestlé or Ghirardelli Semi-Sweet Chocolate Minis

Directions: **Preheat oven to 350 degrees**

1. Sift together dry ingredients. Using a standing mixer with paddle attachment, beat butter, Crisco, and peanut butter together on medium-high until smooth. Add both sugars together and cream mixture until light and fluffy.

2. Add eggs one at a time on medium, beating well after each; stir in vanilla. Scrape bowl and mix again briefly.

3. Gradually add in dry ingredients by large spoonfuls on low; scrape sides and bottom of bowl and continue mixing just until fully incorporated. Stir in all chocolate on low.

4. Scoop dough using a rounded household Tablespoon and roll quickly into balls. Place balls onto parchment-lined cookie sheets, 12 to a pan.

5. **Bake at 350 for 11-12 minutes** until lightly golden brown and just set in the center. Allow cookies to cool on pans for 2 minutes, then slide the parchment onto counter to cool cookies completely.

Makes 30-32 cookies. Can be stored for several days at room temp. (or frozen) in airtight containers.

Peanut Butter Kisses

Such classic cookies! My Peanut Butter Kisses are exceptionally soft and delicious, and these were always a big seller for me. They are my husband Rick's favorite cookies!

Plan ahead as dough must chill overnight (can be made up to two days before).

Ingredients:

3 ¼ cups	Sifted all-purpose flour (Gold Medal pref.), sift first, then measure
2 tsps.	Baking soda
1 tsp.	Salt
1 cup, slightly rounded	Crisco Vegetable Shortening
1 cup, slightly rounded	Skippy Regular Creamy Peanut Butter
1 cup	Domino Sugar

1 cup, packed, slightly rounded	Domino Light Brown Sugar
2 XL	Eggs, room temp.
¼ cup	Whole milk
2 tsps.	Mexican vanilla
1 11-oz. bag	Hershey's Milk Chocolate Kisses

Directions: **Preheat oven to 390 degrees (400 if oven runs low)**

1. Unwrap approx. 50 Kisses. Sift together dry ingredients. Stir vanilla into the milk. Using a standing mixer with paddle attachment, beat Crisco and peanut butter until smooth; add both sugars together, and then cream on medium-high until fluffy.

2. Add eggs one at a time on medium, mixing well after each. Turning mixer to low, add milk mixture in a steady stream. Scrape bowl and mix briefly.

3. Gradually stir in dry ingredients by large spoonfuls on low. Scrape sides and bottom of bowl and continue mixing just until fully incorporated. Chill dough overnight or store in fridge for up to 2 days (actually, baked 2nd day is best).

4. Scoop dough using a *very* rounded household teaspoon and shape into 2-inch balls between your palms. Place balls onto parchment-lined cookie sheets, 15 to a pan.

5. **Bake at 390 for 7.5-8 minutes** until lightly golden brown, puffed, and set. Remove pan from oven and immediately place a Kiss into center of each cookie, pressing down *slightly*. **Bake for an additional 1 minute**. Allow cookies to cool on pans for 2-4 minutes, then slide the parchment onto counter to cool cookies completely (may take 1-1.5 hours for Kisses to harden enough to pack up).

Makes 45-50 cookies. Can be stored for several days (in a single layer) at room temp. in airtight containers.
Freezing is not recommended for the cookies, BUT the dough freezes beautifully!

Pignoli (Pine Nut) Cookies

Naturally Gluten-Free! This is a lighter version of the classic pignoli cookie found in traditional Italian bakeries. Expensive to make, but very special when you do. The orange blossom honey adds a lovely flavor!

Ingredients:

2 8-oz. cans	Solo Pure Almond Paste (do not use almond filling)
1 ½ cups	Domino Confectioners Sugar, sifted
½ tsp.	Salt
2 XL	Egg whites, room temp.
2 Tbs.	Orange blossom honey (organic pref.)
8 - 10 oz.	Pine nuts (raw)

Directions: **Preheat oven to 350 degrees**

1. Line cookie sheets with parchment paper and spray lightly with Pam for Baking, using wax paper to spread it evenly on the parchment.

2. Using a food processor with metal blade insert, pulse the almond paste until broken into small bits. Add sifted confectioners sugar and salt, and process until mixture is finely ground (approx. 1 minute).

3. Transfer almond mixture to a standing mixer bowl and, using paddle attachment, blend in egg whites and honey on medium-high until smooth. Scrape sides of bowl, then continue to mix on medium-high for 5 minutes; chill dough for 30-40 minutes.

4. Transfer slightly chilled dough to a pastry bag with a large plain round tip and pipe 1.5-inch cookies onto prepared pans. Gently press a generous number of pine nuts onto the tops and sides of each cookie. Re-form cookies with your fingertips to ensure that they are still in tall mounds (not flat).

5. **Bake at 350 for 11.5-13 minutes** just until lightly golden on the bottom. Allow cookies to cool on pans for 2 minutes, then slide the parchment onto counter to cool cookies completely. Gently and carefully peel cooled cookies off of parchment paper.

Makes approx. 24 cookies. Can be stored for several days at room temp. (or frozen) in airtight containers.

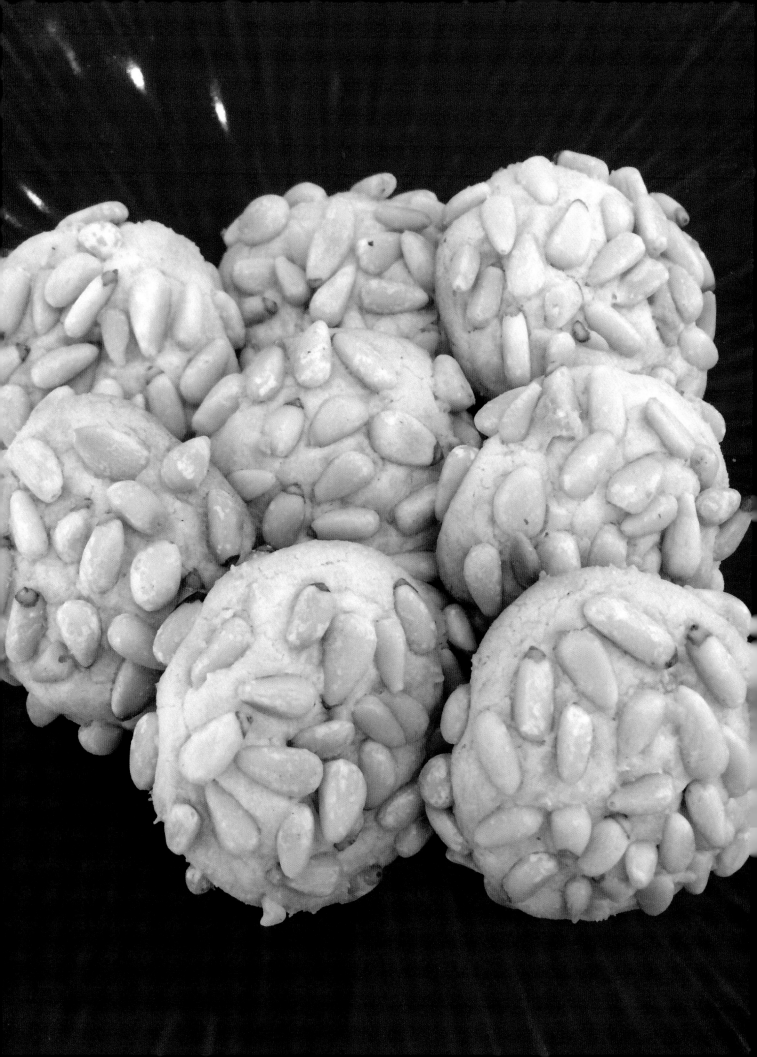

Mary Jane's Pumpkin Cookies

My dear friend Mrs. Mary Jane Carter of Arlington, Virginia, had me make these for her often – they were her favorite cookies, so I named them after her. I've been making this recipe since my oldest son was a toddler, and they continue to be adult Jack's #1 request! These cookies are soft, cake-like, perfectly spiced, lightly drizzled with an orange glaze.

Ingredients:

4 cups	All-purpose flour (Gold Medal pref.)
2 tsps.	Baking powder
2 tsps.	Baking soda
2 tsps., slightly rounded	Cinnamon
½ tsp., scant	Salt
3 dashes each	Nutmeg, Cloves, Ginger
2 dashes	Mexican vanilla
1 cup, slightly rounded	Crisco Vegetable Shortening, room temp.
1 cup	Domino Sugar
1 cup, packed, slightly rounded	Domino Light Brown Sugar
2 cups, slightly rounded	Libby's Pure Pumpkin (measured from 2 reg. size cans or 1 large)
1 Large	Orange for zesting
1 cup, slightly rounded	Golden raisins

Directions: Preheat oven to 375 degrees

1. Sift together dry ingredients. Using a standing mixer with paddle attachment, cream both sugars with Crisco on medium-high until smooth and well blended. Scrape bowl, add pumpkin and orange zest and mix until combined. Stir in vanilla.

2. Gradually mix in dry ingredients by large spoonfuls on low; scrape sides and bottom of bowl and mix again briefly. Gently stir in raisins.

3. Drop dough by very rounded household teaspoons onto parchment-lined cookie sheets, 15 to a pan.

4. **Bake at 375 for 11.5-12 minutes** until very lightly browned, puffed, and set. Allow cookies to cool on pans for 2-3 minutes, then slide the parchment onto counter to cool cookies completely. For best results, chill overnight in airtight containers before icing with Orange Sugar Glaze. May be iced the same day, if necessary.

Orange Sugar Glaze

Ingredients:

2 Tbs.	Unsalted butter (Land O'Lakes pref.), cold, cut into pieces
1 cup	Domino Confectioners Sugar, sifted
1 ½ Tbs.	Whole milk
Dash	Salt
½ tsp.	Orange extract
¼ tsp.	Mexican vanilla

Directions:

1. Melt butter in a double boiler over medium-low heat or set a metal bowl over a pot of 2-inches of simmering water. After the butter has melted, remove from heat and whisk in sifted confectioners sugar, milk, and salt.

2. Return double boiler to low heat, and cook over barely simmering water for 5 minutes, whisking occasionally. Do not overcook. Remove from heat and add in extracts.

3. Transfer glaze to a bowl and whisk to cool down. Add a tiny bit more milk if the glaze seems too thick. Use immediately to decorate cookies when desired consistency has been reached.

4. Glaze can be piped onto pumpkin cookies or drizzled on with a spoon. Allow glaze to harden before moving cookies to airtight containers or well-wrapped platters.

Makes 48-50 cookies. Can be stored for several days at room temp. in airtight containers.
Can be frozen before being glazed.

Soft Sugar Cookies

Always popular during my Holiday Cookie Carousels and Super Bowl Specials. Mine are soft and more delicate than other sugar cookies. And the hint of almond in the icing makes them extra special.

Plan ahead as these take time and patience! Three days start to finish!

Ingredients:

2 ½ cups	All-purpose flour (Gold Medal pref.)
1 tsp.	Baking powder
½ tsp.	Salt
1 ½ cups	Domino Confectioners Sugar, sifted
1 cup (2 sticks)	Unsalted butter (Land O'Lakes pref.), very soft
1 XL	Egg, room temp.
1 XL	Egg yolk
1 Tbs.	Mexican vanilla
2 cups	Confectioners sugar, sifted
2 Tbs. + 2 tsps.	Whole Milk
2 Tbs.	Unsalted butter, very soft
2 tsps.	Vanilla
⅓ tsp.	Almond extract (Nielsen-Massey pref.)

Directions:

Dough/Day 1:

1. Sift together dry ingredients. Using a standing mixer with paddle attachment, cream the sifted confectioners sugar and butter on medium until light and fluffy. Turning the mixer to low, beat in egg and egg yolk, then add vanilla. Scrape bowl and mix.

2. Gradually add in dry ingredients by large spoonfuls on low, mixing until just combined. Scrape sides and bottom of bowl and mix again very briefly.

3. Divide dough into two flat disks, wrap in plastic, let rest for 30 minutes, then chill dough overnight.

Baking/Day 2: **Preheat oven to 325 degrees**

1. Set dough out for approx. 30 minutes. Using a rolling pin on a large flat surface, roll the dough between two sheets of plastic wrap (dusted with a bit of flour) to approx. 1/4-inch thickness. Wrap each rolled-out disk in plastic, lay them flat on a cookie sheet, and place pan in freezer as you continue to work with the rest of the dough. Repeat this process until you've rolled out all of it.

2. Working quickly, cut cookies out of slightly frozen dough and place on parchment-lined cookie sheets, spaced 2-inches apart (cookies will expand during baking!). Gather dough scraps, re-form into a disk, and chill or freeze until you can roll this out for more cookies. Keep repeating this process until you've used all of the dough.

3. **Bake at 325 for 8.5-9 minutes for small shapes (9.5-10 minutes for large ones)** just until cookies are set and slightly golden at the edges. Allow cookies to cool on pans for 2 minutes, then slide the parchment onto counter to cool cookies completely. Store cookies overnight in airtight containers before decorating.

Decorating/Day 3:

Almond Icing:

Sift confectioners sugar into a large bowl, whisk in milk, very soft butter, and extracts. Whisk until spreadable, adding a bit more milk if icing seems too thick.

Separate icing into several small bowls if you'd like to use food dyes or gels to make different colors. Use piping bags with a variety of small tips to decorate as you like. Decorations must be used on top of the icing while it is still wet, so only decorate a few cookies at a time!

Makes 35-50 cookies depending on the shape. Decorated cookies can be stored for several days at room temp. in airtight containers or well-wrapped platters.

Cookies can be frozen until ready to ice/decorate.

Steel-Cut Oatmeal Cookies

with White Chocolate and Cherries

I designed this recipe for the café at Bards Alley Bookstore. The cardamom makes these cookies special, and the steel-cut oats give them a superb texture. Fantastic when you want a cookie that's unique but easy to make!

Ingredients:

1 cup	All-purpose flour (Gold Medal pref.)
½ tsp.	Baking powder
½ tsp.	Salt
¼ tsp., slightly rounded	Cinnamon
¼ tsp., slightly rounded	Nutmeg
⅛ tsp., slightly rounded	Cardamom
1 cup	Quaker Oats Steel Cut Quick 3-Minute Oats
½ cup (1 stick)	Unsalted butter (Land O'Lakes pref.), room temp.
¼ cup, level	Domino Sugar
½ cup, packed, slightly rounded	Domino Light Brown Sugar
1 XL	Egg, room temp.
¾ tsp.	Mexican vanilla
½ cup	Nestlé White Chocolate chips
½ cup	Dried cherries (organic pref.)

Directions: **Preheat oven to 350 degrees**

1. Sift together dry ingredients directly into a large bowl, add oats and mix with a fork until combined. Using a standing mixer with paddle attachment, beat butter briefly, then cream together with both sugars on medium-high until fluffy and smooth.

2. Blend in the egg, then vanilla, with mixer on medium. Scrape bowl and mix briefly.

3. Gradually add in dry ingredients by large spoonfuls on low. Scrape bowl and continue mixing until fully incorporated; stir in white chocolate chips and cherries.

4. Scoop dough using a rounded household Tablespoon and roll quickly into balls. Place balls onto parchment-lined cookie sheets, 9 to a pan (press down lightly on each to flatten slightly).

5. **Bake at 350 for 12-13 minutes** until edges are golden. Allow cookies to cool on pans for 2 minutes, then slide the parchment onto counter to cool cookies completely.

Makes 20-22 cookies. Can be stored for two to three days at room temp. (or frozen) in airtight containers.

Triple Trouble Chocolate Cookies

Chocolaty, chewy, and super moist, these often appeared on my Cookie Carousel Specials (and at Marshall High School baseball games!).

Plan ahead as dough must chill overnight.

Ingredients:

2 oz.	Baker's Unsweetened Chocolate, chopped
8 oz.	Nestlé Semi-Sweet Chocolate chips
6 Tbs. (¾ stick)	Unsalted butter (Land O'Lakes pref.), cold, cut into pieces
3 Tbs.	Hershey's Cocoa Powder
1 ½ tsps.	Mexican vanilla
1 cup	All-purpose flour (Gold Medal pref.)
1 tsp.	Baking powder

¾ tsp.	Salt
3 XL	Eggs, room temp.
1 cup, slightly rounded	Domino Sugar
½ cup	Nestlé Semi-Sweet Chocolate chips
½ cup	Nestlé White Chocolate chips
½ cup	Walnuts, chopped (optional)

Directions: **Preheat oven to 350 degrees**

1. Melt both chocolates with butter in a double boiler over medium-low heat or set a metal bowl over a pot of 2-inches of simmering water; when melted, whisk until smooth. Immediately whisk in cocoa to "melt" off heat. Cool slightly, then add vanilla.

2. Sift together dry ingredients. Combine dark and white chips in a small bowl.

3. Using a standing mixer with whisk attachment, beat eggs and add sugar in a steady stream, mixing on medium-high until frothy and starting to thicken. Switching to paddle attachment, blend in chocolate mixture on low, scrape bowl, and mix well.

4. Gradually add in dry ingredients by large spoonfuls on low until just combined (do not overbeat). Stir in both chips (and nuts, if using). Chill dough overnight.

5. Scoop dough using a slightly heaping household teaspoon, then roll between (slightly dampened) palms into balls. Place balls 2-inches apart on parchment-lined cookie sheets, 12 to a pan.

6. **Bake at 350 for 11-12 minutes** until cookies are puffed, set, but still soft in the center. Allow cookies to cool on pans for 2 minutes, then slide the parchment onto counter to cool cookies completely.

Makes approx. 28 cookies. Can be stored for several days at room temp. in airtight containers.
These freeze particularly well!

Break My Heart Brownies

Classic and very moist. Mine have crackled tops and very soft centers. They had a loyal following with many of my customers regardless of age! And were always a big seller at Bards Alley Bookstore & Café!

Plan ahead as these need to sit overnight before cutting.

Ingredients:

2 oz.	Baker's Unsweetened Chocolate, chopped
8 oz.	Nestlé Semi-Sweet Chocolate chips
1 cup (2 sticks)	Unsalted butter (Land O'Lakes pref.) cold, cut into pieces
1 cup	All-purpose flour (Gold Medal pref.)
1 tsp.	Baking powder
½ tsp., slightly rounded	Salt
5 XL	Eggs, room temp.
1 ½ cups	Domino Sugar
1 ½ tsps.	Mexican vanilla

Directions: **Preheat oven to 350 degrees**

1. Melt both chocolates with butter in a double boiler over medium-low heat or set a metal bowl over a pot of 2-inches of simmering water; when melted, whisk until smooth. Cool slightly, then add vanilla.

2. Grease a 13x9-inch metal pan with Crisco and line with parchment paper. Sift together dry ingredients.

3. Using a standing mixer with whisk attachment, beat eggs briefly. Add sugar in a steady stream and beat mixture on medium-high until light in color, thickened, and increased in volume (1.5-2 minutes).

4. Switching to paddle attachment, gently mix in dry ingredients on low, then add slightly warm chocolate mixture until just combined. Scrape bowl and mix briefly. Pour batter into prepared pan and even out top gently with a spatula if needed.

5. **Bake at 350 for 27-28 minutes** until puffed, just set, with one significant crack running through the center. Place brownies on a wire rack to cool completely (2-2.5 hours); cover tightly with Press'n Seal, then foil. Store at room temp. overnight. Remove edges before cutting as desired, then dust with confectioners sugar (through a fine-mesh strainer) just before serving.

Makes 24 square or 12 heart-shaped brownies.

Can be stored for several days at room temp. (or frozen) in airtight containers.

Brown Butter Blondies

Super moist, dotted with white chocolate and coconut. Brown butter is the secret ingredient! These are a fun treat when you want something a bit different, and they are super easy to make!

Plan ahead as these need to sit overnight before cutting.

Ingredients:

1 cup (2 sticks)	Unsalted butter (Land O'Lakes pref.), cold, cut into pieces
1 ½ cups	All-purpose flour (Gold Medal pref.)
1 tsp.	Baking powder
½ tsp.	Salt
½ cup	Domino Sugar
1 cup, packed, slightly rounded	Domino Light Brown Sugar
2 XL	Eggs, room temp.
2 tsps.	Mexican vanilla

1 Tbs.	Fresh lemon juice
½ cup	Baker's Angel Flake Sweetened Coconut
½ cup	Nestlé White Chocolate chips

Directions: **Preheat oven to 325 degrees**

1. In a small pot, clarify butter by melting on low then pulling off heat to let milk solids rise to the top; skim off solids and discard. Measure out ⅔ cup of clarified butter and pour into a heavy-bottomed pot.

2. Brown on medium heat for 5 minutes until butter turns a pretty nut-brown color, carefully swirling the butter during this process. This can go from perfect to ruined very quickly! Pull off heat and pour immediately into a bowl (be sure to use a spatula to scrape up all the brown bits on the bottom) to cool slightly once desired color has been reached.

3. Grease an 8-inch square metal pan with Crisco and line with parchment paper. Sift together dry ingredients.

4. Using a standing mixer with paddle attachment, cream both sugars with browned butter on medium-high until thoroughly combined. Add eggs one at a time on low, beating well after each. Scrape bowl, add vanilla and lemon juice, and mix until just blended.

5. Gradually add in dry ingredients on low, then stir in coconut and white chocolate. Scoop dough into prepared pan, smoothing top with a rubber spatula (batter will be very thick).

6. **Bake at 325 for 45 minutes** until top is golden brown and tester comes out clean. Place bars on a wire rack to cool completely (2 hours); cover tightly with Press'n Seal, then foil. Store at room temp. overnight. Remove edges before cutting as desired. These are quite rich, so cut them on the small side!

Makes 20-24 small rectangles.

Can be stored for several days at room temp. (or frozen) in airtight containers.

Amaretto Cheesecake Brownie Bites

An adult taste profile for these moist and delicious bars. This recipe makes a lot of "bites" - wonderful for a party!

Plan ahead as these need to chill overnight before cutting.

Ingredients:

1 oz.	Baker's Unsweetened Chocolate, chopped
7 oz.	Nestlé Semi-Sweet Chocolate chips
½ cup (1 stick)	Unsalted butter (Land O'Lakes pref.), cold, cut into pieces
1 ½ cups	Domino Sugar
4 XL	Eggs, room temp.
2 tsps.	Mexican vanilla

1 ¼ cups	All-purpose flour (Gold Medal pref.)
¾ tsp.	Baking powder
½ tsp.	Salt
12 oz.	Regular cream cheese (Philadelphia brand pref.), softened
½ cup	Sugar
2 Tbs.	Disaronno Amaretto
¾ tsp.	Vanilla
¼ tsp.	Almond extract (Nielsen-Massey pref.)
1 XL	Egg, room temp.

Directions: **Preheat oven to 350 degrees**

1. Melt both chocolates with butter in a double boiler over medium-low heat or set a metal bowl over a pot of 2-inches of simmering water; when melted, whisk until smooth. Cool slightly.

2. Grease a 13x9-inch metal pan with Crisco and line with parchment paper. Sift together dry ingredients.

3. Transfer chocolate mixture to a large bowl and whisk in 1 ½ cups sugar vigorously by hand until well combined; whisk in eggs one at a time, then add vanilla.

4. Gently fold in dry ingredients in two additions using a large rubber spatula, being sure to scrape along edges and bottom of bowl.

5. Using a standing mixer with whisk attachment, beat cream cheese on medium-high until smooth; gradually add ½ cup sugar with mixer on low. Add Amaretto, vanilla, and almond extract, then egg, and continue to beat until smooth and well combined. Scrape bowl and mix briefly.

6. Spread approx. two-thirds of the chocolate batter into prepared pan; spoon cream cheese batter on top in large dollops, then spoon remaining chocolate batter on top of that. With a thin metal spatula or knife, draw through all three layers starting end to end lengthwise, then across, in 1 - 2 repetitions until you have a nice "marbling" effect.

7. **Bake at 350 for 34-36 minutes** until tester comes out with moist crumbs attached. Place bars on a wire rack to cool completely (2-2.5 hours); cover tightly with Press'n Seal, then foil. Store overnight in fridge. Remove edges before cutting as desired. Allow brownie bites to sit out at room temp. 1.5-2 hours before serving for best taste and texture.

Makes approx. 40 small bites.

Can be stored for several days in the fridge (or frozen) in airtight containers.

Mint Cheesecake Brownie Bites

So easy and fun to make – perfect when you only need a little bite of something sweet. Love the subtlety of the mint with the dark chocolate in this one!

Plan ahead as these need to chill overnight before cutting.

Ingredients:

1 oz.	Baker's Unsweetened Chocolate, chopped
7 oz.	Nestlé Semi-Sweet Chocolate chips
½ cup (1 stick)	Unsalted butter (Land O'Lakes pref.), cold, cut into pieces
1 ½ cups	Domino Sugar
4 XL	Eggs, room temp.
2 tsps.	Mexican vanilla
1 ¼ cups	All-purpose flour (Gold Medal pref.)

¾ tsp.	Baking powder
½ tsp.	Salt
12 oz.	Regular cream cheese (Philadelphia brand pref.), softened
½ cup + 2 Tbs.	Sugar
1 XL	Egg, room temp.
2 Tbs.	Crème de Menthe White Liqueur
¾ tsp.	Mint extract
	Or if not using liqueur:
½ tsp.	Peppermint extract
1 tsp.	Mint extract

Directions: Preheat oven to 350 degrees

1. Melt both chocolates with butter in a double boiler over medium-low heat or set a metal bowl over a pot of 2-inches of simmering water; when melted, whisk until smooth. Cool slightly.

2. Grease a 13x9-inch metal pan with Crisco and line with parchment paper. Sift together dry ingredients.

3. Transfer chocolate mixture to a large bowl and whisk in 1 ½ cups sugar vigorously by hand until well combined; whisk in eggs one at a time, then add vanilla.

4. Gently fold in dry ingredients in two additions using a large rubber spatula, being sure to scrape along edges and bottom of bowl.

5. Using a standing mixer with whisk attachment, beat cream cheese on medium-high until smooth; gradually add ½ cup + 2 Tbs. sugar with mixer on low. Add mint liqueur (if using) and mint extract(s), then egg, and continue to beat until smooth and well combined. Scrape bowl and mix briefly.

6. Spread approx. two-thirds of the chocolate batter into prepared pan; spoon cream cheese batter on top in large dollops, then spoon remaining chocolate batter on top of that. With a thin metal spatula or knife, draw through all three layers starting end to end lengthwise, then across, in 1 - 2 repetitions until you have a nice "marbling" effect.

7. **Bake at 350 for 34-36 minutes** until tester comes out with moist crumbs attached. Place bars on wire rack to cool completely (2-2.5 hours); cover tightly with Press'n Seal, then foil. Store overnight in fridge. Remove edges before cutting as desired. Allow brownie bites to sit out at room temp. 1.5-2 hours before serving for best taste and texture.

Makes approx. 40 small bites.

Can be stored for several days in the fridge (or frozen) in airtight containers.

Vanilla Cheesecake Brownie Bites

These make-ahead treats appeal to both kids and adults!

Plan ahead as these need to chill overnight before cutting.

Ingredients:

1 oz.	Baker's Unsweetened Chocolate, chopped
7 oz.	Nestlé Semi-Sweet Chocolate chips
½ cup (1 stick)	Unsalted butter (Land O'Lakes pref.), cold, cut into pieces
1 ½ cups	Domino Sugar
4 XL	Eggs, room temp.
2 tsps.	Mexican vanilla
1 ¼ cups	All-purpose flour (Gold Medal pref.)

¾ tsp.	Baking powder
½ tsp.	Salt
12 oz.	Regular cream cheese (Philadelphia brand pref.), softened
½ cup	Sugar
1 Tbs.	Vanilla
2 tsps.	Heavy whipping cream
1 XL	Egg, room temp.

Directions: Preheat oven to 350 degrees

1. Melt both chocolates with butter in a double boiler over medium-low heat or set a metal bowl over a pot of 2-inches of simmering water; when melted, whisk until smooth. Cool slightly.

2. Grease a 13x9-inch metal pan with Crisco and line with parchment paper. Sift together dry ingredients.

3. Transfer chocolate mixture to a large bowl and whisk in 1 ½ cups sugar vigorously by hand until well combined; whisk in eggs one at a time, then add vanilla.

4. Gently fold in dry ingredients in two additions using a large rubber spatula, being sure to scrape along edges and bottom of bowl.

5. Using a standing mixer with whisk attachment, beat cream cheese on medium-high until smooth; gradually add ½ cup sugar with mixer on low. Add vanilla, cream, then egg, and continue to beat until smooth and well combined. Scrape bowl and mix briefly.

6. Spread approx. two-thirds of the chocolate batter into prepared pan; spoon cream cheese batter on top in large dollops, then spoon remaining chocolate batter on top of that. With a thin metal spatula or knife, draw through all three layers starting end to end lengthwise, then across, in 1 - 2 repetitions until you have a nice "marbling" effect.

7. **Bake at 350 for 34-36 minutes** until tester comes out with moist crumbs attached. Place bars on a wire rack to cool completely (2-2.5 hours); cover tightly with Press'n Seal, then foil. Store overnight in fridge. Remove edges before cutting as desired. Allow brownie bites to sit out at room temp. 1.5-2 hours before serving for best taste and texture.

Makes approx. 40 small bites.

Can be stored for several days in the fridge (or frozen) in airtight containers.

Mary Lee's Famous M&M Bars

My recipe was included in The Washington Post's Annual Holiday Cookie Issue in December 2011 and became the most viewed/downloaded of <u>any</u> online recipe in The Post for all of 2012! It was re-published in The Post's Food Section in November 2020.

Plan ahead as these need to sit overnight before cutting.

Ingredients:

2 ¾ cups	All-purpose flour (Gold Medal pref.)
2 tsps.	Baking powder
1 tsp.	Salt
½ cup (1 stick)	Unsalted butter (Land O'Lakes pref.), room temp.
½ cup, slightly rounded	Crisco Vegetable Shortening, room temp.
½ cup, rounded	Domino Sugar
1 cup, packed, slightly rounded	Domino Light Brown Sugar
3 XL	Eggs, room temp.
4 tsps.	Mexican vanilla
2 Tbs., slightly rounded	Regular sour cream (Breakstone's or similar)
12 oz.	M&M's Milk Chocolate Candies

Directions: **Preheat oven to 350 degrees**

1. Grease a 13x9-inch metal pan with Crisco and line with parchment paper. Sift together dry ingredients.

2. Using a standing mixer with paddle attachment, beat butter and Crisco together on medium-high until smooth; add both sugars together and cream mixture until light and fluffy.

3. Add eggs one at a time on medium, beating well after each. Blend in sour cream and vanilla, scrape bowl, and mix again briefly.

4. Gradually add in dry ingredients by large spoonfuls on low; scrape sides and bottom of bowl and continue mixing just until fully incorporated. Gently stir in M&M's by hand or on low. Scoop dough into prepared pan and smooth top with a large rubber spatula.

5. **Bake at 350 for 26-27 minutes** until lightly golden, then cover loosely with heavy-duty foil and **bake another 7-9 minutes** until center is puffed, barely set, and springs back when lightly touched. Place bars on a wire rack to cool completely (2-2.5 hours); cover tightly with Press'n Seal, then foil. Store at room temp. overnight. Remove edges before cutting as desired.

Makes approx. 24 bars. Can be stored for several days at room temp. (or frozen) in airtight containers.

Snickerdoodle Bars

I love the taste of classic Snickerdoodles, but the cookies don't stay fresh for long....so I reimagined them as a delicious bar, and they sold well at Bards Alley Bookstore & Café. Mine are thick, moist, with a big cinnamon taste....and they last for days!

Plan ahead as these need to sit overnight before cutting.

Ingredients:

4 Tbs.	Domino Sugar
2 tsps., slightly rounded	Cinnamon
⅛ tsp., slightly rounded	Nutmeg
2 ⅔ cups	All-purpose flour (Gold Medal pref.)
2 tsps.	Baking powder
¾ tsp.	Salt
1 cup (2 sticks)	Unsalted butter (Land O'Lakes pref.), room temp.
1 cup, level	Sugar
1 cup, packed, slightly rounded	Domino Light Brown Sugar
2 XL	Eggs, room temp.
2 tsps.	Mexican vanilla

Directions: **Preheat oven to 350 degrees**

1. In a small bowl, mix sugar, cinnamon, and nutmeg with a fork and set aside. Grease a 13x9-inch metal pan with Crisco and line with parchment paper. Sift together dry ingredients.

2. Using a standing mixer with paddle attachment, beat butter briefly, then add both sugars together; cream on medium-high until fluffy and smooth.

3. Add eggs one at a time on medium, beating well after each; add vanilla. Scrape bowl and mix briefly.

4. Gradually add in dry ingredients by large spoonfuls on low; scrape sides and bottom of bowl and continue mixing just until fully incorporated (dough will be very thick). Scoop dough into prepared pan and smooth top with a large rubber spatula. Sprinkle cinnamon-sugar mixture liberally and evenly all over the top (use all of it).

5. **Bake at 350 for 29-30 minutes** until golden and center is set when touched. Place bars on a wire rack to cool completely (2-2.5 hours); cover tightly with Press'n Seal, then foil. Store at room temp. overnight. Remove edges before cutting as desired.

Makes approx. 24 bars. Can be stored at room temp. for several days (or frozen) in airtight containers.

Tartlets!

Mini Amaretto Italian Cheesecakes

Mini Triple Sec Italian Cheesecakes

Mini Key Lime Pies

Fancy Lemon Tartlets

Peanut Butter Brownie Cups

Aunt Johnnie's Pecan Tassies

Mini Amaretto Italian Cheesecakes

These are lovely little tartlets: easy to make and so delicious. This recipe makes a lot of mini cheesecakes – perfect for parties!

Ingredients:

¾ cup	Honey Maid Graham Cracker Crumbs
2 Tbs.	Domino Sugar
2 Tbs.	Unsalted butter (Land O'Lakes pref.), melted
15 oz. (1 cont.)	Whole milk ricotta (Galbani or Polly-O pref.)
8 oz.	Regular cream cheese (Philadelphia brand pref.), softened
½ cup	Sugar
2 Tbs.	Heavy whipping cream
⅓ cup	Disaronno Amaretto (in combination with cream to make ⅓ cup)
⅛ tsp.	Almond extract (Nielsen & Massey pref.)
1 tsp.	Mexican vanilla
¼ tsp.	Salt
4 XL	Eggs, room temp., lightly beaten

Directions: **Preheat oven to 325 degrees**

1. While oven is preheating, place a shallow roasting pan of hot water on bottom rack of oven and leave it there during baking (creates steam for your cheesecakes).

2. For the crust, combine crumbs, sugar, and melted butter in a bowl and mix with a fork until well combined. Line mini muffin pans with mini paper cupcake liners, then place a ¾ measuring teaspoon of crumb mixture inside each; press down gently on crust with back of a rounded measuring teaspoon.

3. Using a food processor with metal blade insert, beat ricotta for 2 minutes until smooth. Add cream cheese and continue to blend, scraping sides of bowl, then add sugar and process until mixture is very smooth.

4. Measure cream into a ⅓ cup dry measuring cup, then fill to the top with Amaretto. Blend this into the cream cheese mixture along with extracts and salt; mix eggs in last. (Mixture can be made up to 1 hour ahead and chilled if needed).

5. Using a glass measuring cup, pour cheesecake batter into each tartlet cup, filling to the top. **Bake at 325 for 24-25 minutes** until puffed and set. Cool in pans until you can remove them easily to cool completely on wire racks. Must be chilled until ready to serve. Best served cold.

Makes 50-55 mini cheesecakes. Can be stored for several days, chilled, in airtight containers. Cannot be frozen.

DISARONNO®

ORIGINALE

SINCE 1525

THE WORLD'S FAVORITE
ITALIAN LIQUEUR

A LIQUEUR PRODUCED BY
ILLVA · SARONNO · ITALY

28% ALC. BY VOL. 375 ML

Mini Triple Sec Italian Cheesecakes

The Triple Sec liqueur in this recipe gives a surprising pop of citrus! (Note: the liqueur and cream are balanced differently here than in the Amaretto version). These can be topped with a single berry or a strawberry slice.

Ingredients:

¾ cup	Honey Maid Graham Cracker Crumbs
2 Tbs.	Domino Sugar
2 Tbs.	Unsalted butter (Land O'Lakes pref.), melted
15 oz. (1 cont.)	Whole milk ricotta (Galbani or Polly-O pref.)
8 oz.	Regular cream cheese (Philadelphia brand pref.), softened
½ cup	Sugar
2 ½ Tbs.	Triple Sec liqueur
⅓ cup	Heavy whipping cream (in combination with Triple Sec to make ⅓ cup)
¼ tsp.	Orange extract

¼ tsp.	Lemon extract
¼ tsp.	Mexican vanilla
Dash	Salt
4 XL	Eggs, room temp., lightly beaten

Directions: Preheat oven to 325 degrees

1. While oven is preheating, place a shallow roasting pan of hot water on bottom rack of oven and leave it there during baking (creates steam for your cheesecakes).

2. For the crust, combine crumbs, sugar, and melted butter in a bowl and mix with a fork until well combined. Line mini muffin pans with mini paper cupcake liners, then place a ¾ measuring teaspoon of crumb mixture inside each; press down gently on crust with back of a rounded measuring teaspoon.

3. Using a food processor with metal blade insert, beat ricotta for 2 minutes until smooth. Add cream cheese and continue to blend, scraping sides of bowl, then add sugar and process until mixture is very smooth.

4. Measure Triple Sec into a ⅓ cup dry measuring cup, then fill to the top with cream. Blend this into the cream cheese mixture along with extracts and salt; mix eggs in last. (Mixture can be made up to 1 hour ahead and chilled if needed).

5. Using a glass measuring cup, pour cheesecake batter into each tartlet cup, filling to the top. **Bake at 325 for 24-25 minutes** until puffed and set. Cool in pans until you can remove them easily to cool completely on wire racks. Must be chilled until ready to serve. Best served cold.

Makes 50-55 mini cheesecakes. Can be stored for several days, chilled, in airtight containers.

Cannot be frozen.

Mini Key Lime Pies

These are delicious and elegant looking tartlets and so easy to make. These were always very popular with customers and at home! This recipe makes a lot – perfect for a party!

Plan ahead as these must chill overnight before being finished with stabilized whipped cream.

Ingredients:

½ cup + 2 Tbs.	Honey Maid Graham Cracker Crumbs
2 Tbs.	Domino Sugar
2 ½ Tbs.	Unsalted butter (Land O'Lakes pref.), melted
8 XL	Egg yolks, room temp.
2 14-oz. cans	Sweetened condensed milk (Eagle brand pref.)
1 cup	Nellie & Joe's Key West Lime Juice
½ Small	Lime for zesting
1 cup	Heavy whipping cream (not organic)

1 Tbs.	Regular sour cream (Breakstone's or similar)
1 ½ Tbs.	Sugar (granulated)
1 ½ Tbs.	Domino Confectioners Sugar
1 tsp.	Mexican vanilla

Directions: **Preheat oven to 350 degrees**

1. For the crust: combine crumbs, sugar, and melted butter in a bowl and mix with a fork until well combined. Line mini muffin pans with mini paper cupcake liners, then place a ¾ (measuring) teaspoon of crumb mixture inside each; press down gently on crust with back of a rounded (measuring) teaspoon.

2. In a large bowl, whisk yolks vigorously by hand, add condensed milk, lime juice, and zest, whisking well after each until the filling is smooth and thickened. Using a glass measuring cup, pour key lime filling into each tartlet cup nearly to the top.

3. **Bake at 350 for 16-17 minutes** until just set (do not allow to crack). Cool in pans for approx. 15 minutes, then carefully remove each tartlet to wire racks to cool completely. Chill overnight before finishing with stabilized whipped cream.

Whipped cream:

Chill bowl and whisk attachment of standing mixer in freezer. Mix both sugars in a small bowl with a fork. Beat cream and sour cream on medium-high briefly, then turn mixer to low to add sugars and vanilla. Increase speed to high and whip until stiff peaks form (do not overbeat). Using a pastry bag with a large star tip, decorate the tops of each well-chilled tartlet by pulling straight up to create a big star. Chill tartlets until ready to serve. Can be brought out 30 minutes before serving or served cold.

Makes 48-54 tartlets. Can be stored for one to two days in the fridge in airtight containers.

Cannot be frozen.

Fancy Lemon Tartlets

These are perfect for special occasions. Super elegant, smooth, and lemony. They take a lot of effort to make, but they are worth it! For a little cheat, you can use high-quality pre-made tart shells. The wow factor in this recipe is the homemade lemon mousse!

Plan ahead as you'll need two to three days to make these!

Ingredients:

3 cups	Sifted all-purpose flour (Gold Medal pref.), (sift first, then measure)
½ cup	Domino Sugar
2 Large	Lemons for zesting
1 cup (2 sticks)	Unsalted butter (Land O'Lakes pref.), cold, cut into cubes
2 XL	Eggs, slightly beaten
¼ cup (½ stick)	Unsalted butter, cold, cut into pieces
¼ cup + 2 Tbs.	Sugar
¼ cup	Fresh lemon juice
Dash	Salt
3 XL	Egg yolks, slightly beaten
1 cup	Heavy whipping cream (not organic)
1 ½ Tbs.	Sugar (granulated)
1 ½ Tbs.	Domino Confectioners Sugar
1 cup	Heavy whipping cream (not organic)
1 Tbs.	Regular sour cream (Breakstone's or similar)
1 ½ Tbs.	Sugar (granulated)
1 ½ Tbs.	Confectioners sugar
1 tsp.	Mexican vanilla

Directions:

Tart Dough/ Day 1:

1. Mix the first three ingredients (flour, sugar, zest) in a food processor with metal blade insert and pulse until combined. Add cold butter a few cubes at a time through the tube opening, then pulse until it is just incorporated (coarse crumbs formed).

2. Add beaten eggs and pulse for several seconds until dough masses; scrape sides of bowl and pulse once or twice. Form dough into a disk, wrap in plastic, let rest for 30 minutes, then chill for 1.5 hours.

3. Lightly spray mini muffin pans with Pam for Baking. Roll dough into small 1-inch balls (flour fingertips if needed), then press dough evenly onto bottom and up sides of each tartlet cup, making sure that bottom and sides are not too thick (avoid bare spots). Using your fingertips, smooth the dough around each cup's "lip". Freeze pan for 3 minutes, then prick the bottom of each dough cup with a fork.

4. **Bake at 350 for 16 minutes** until just golden in color; flip immediately onto a large cookie sheet, then place cups on wire racks to cool completely. Store at room temp. in airtight containers.

Lemon Mousse/Day 2:

1. Chill bowl and whisk attachment of standing mixer in freezer. Stir together both sugars in a small bowl with a fork.

2. Melt butter in a medium size, heavy-bottomed pot over low heat. Remove from heat and whisk in sugar, lemon juice, and salt by hand. Then whisk in yolks until smooth.

3. Return pot to stove and cook, whisking over medium heat until thick and an instant-read thermometer reaches 165 degrees (should leave a path on back of a wooden spoon). Do not allow to boil.

4. Pour lemon curd immediately through a mesh strainer set over a glass bowl; cover with plastic wrap and allow to cool almost to room temp. (still a little warm).

5. Using the chilled bowl and whisk attachment, whip heavy cream with both sugars until stiff peaks form. Using a large rubber spatula, fold whipped cream into slightly warm curd in 3 - 4 additions. Chill lemon mousse well wrapped overnight in fridge.

Final Assembly/Day 3:

1. Chill bowl and whisk attachment of standing mixer in freezer. Stir together both sugars in a small bowl with a fork.

2. Fill tart shells by piping chilled lemon mousse decoratively into pastry cups using a medium star tip, swirling to fill each.

3. Using the chilled bowl and whisk attachment, beat cream and sour cream on medium-high briefly, then turn mixer to low to add sugars and vanilla. Increase speed to high and whip until stiff peaks form (do not overbeat).

4. Place whipped cream inside a pastry bag with a very small star tip to decorate each tartlet as desired. Tartlets must be chilled until ready to serve. Best served cold.

Makes 50-60 tartlets. Best served the day of completion but can be stored one to two days in the fridge in airtight containers. Cannot be frozen.

Peanut Butter Brownie Cups

These are fun little two-bite desserts, just right for any occasion.

I've made these for Super Bowl Specials and weddings!

Ingredients:

6 oz.	Nestlé Semi-Sweet Chocolate chips
⅓ cup (⅔ stick)	Unsalted butter (Land O'Lakes pref.),cold, cut into pieces
½ cup	All-purpose flour (Gold Medal pref.)
½ tsp.	Baking powder
¼ tsp.	Salt
2 XL	Eggs, room temp.
½ cup	Domino Sugar
1 tsp.	Mexican vanilla
1 cup, rounded	Reese's Miniature Peanut Butter Cups (22-24 cups), unwrapped then chilled

Directions: **Preheat oven to 350 degrees**

1. Melt chocolate with butter in a double boiler over medium-low heat or set a metal bowl over a pot of 2-inches of simmering water; when melted, whisk until smooth. Cool slightly, then add vanilla.

2. Sift together dry ingredients. Roughly chop chilled peanut butter cups and set aside.

3. Using a standing mixer with whisk attachment, beat eggs briefly, then add sugar in a steady stream with mixer on medium-low. Turn mixer to medium-high and beat mixture until light in color, thickened, and increased in volume (1.5-2 minutes).

4. Switch to paddle attachment and gently mix in dry ingredients on low. Add in chocolate mixture and mix until just combined. Scrape bowl well and mix again briefly; gently fold in chopped peanut butter cups by hand with a large rubber spatula.

5. Lightly spray mini muffin pans with Pam for Baking; fill each tartlet cup nearly to the top (using a measuring teaspoon to scoop batter is easiest).

6. **Bake at 350 for 11-12 minutes** until puffy and centers are set. Cool 15 minutes in pans, then tilt over a large cookie sheet to release (may need a good shake!). Cool brownie cups completely on wire racks. Best served at room temp.

Makes 18-22 brownie cups (allowing for breakage). Can be stored for several days at room temp. (or frozen) in airtight containers. The tops are very delicate, so only store these in a single layer!

Photo by Anna Grace Photography, LLC

Aunt Johnnie's Pecan Tassies

I adapted this recipe from my Aunt Johnnie Mae Berry's of Kentucky. These were one of her specialties, and she made them often. Like tiny pecan pies - always very popular with my customers during the holidays!

Dough can be made one day before if needed.

Ingredients:

8 oz.	Regular cream cheese (Philadelphia brand pref.), softened
1 cup (2 sticks)	Unsalted butter (Land O'Lakes pref.), very soft
2 cups	Sifted all-purpose flour (Gold Medal pref.), sift first, then measure
2 XL	Eggs, room temp.
1 ½ cups, packed, slightly rounded	Domino Dark Brown Sugar
2 Tbs.	Unsalted butter, very soft

2 tsps.	Mexican vanilla
Pinch	Salt
1 ⅓ cups, slightly rounded	Whole pecans (measure first, then chop)

Directions: **Preheat oven to 325 degrees**

1. Using a standing mixer with paddle attachment, blend cream cheese and butter on medium-high until smooth. Add flour by large spoonfuls on low and mix until just combined. Scrape bowl and mix briefly. Removing dough to counter, gently fold it over on itself several times; pat into a disk, wrap tightly, and chill for 1 hour.

2. Place pecans on a plate and discard any with dark spots or shells. In a food processor with metal insert, pulse nuts until somewhat fine (a few small pieces are ok). In a medium bowl, whisk eggs vigorously by hand with brown sugar until well combined, then add soft butter, vanilla, salt, and whisk until smooth. Stir in chopped nuts.

3. Lightly spray mini muffin pans with Pam for Baking. Roll dough into small 1-inch balls (flour fingertips if needed). Press dough evenly onto bottom and up sides of each tartlet cup, making sure that it is not too thick (avoid bare spots). Using your fingertips, smooth the dough around each cup's "lip".

4. Using a measuring teaspoon, fill each cup nearly to the top (be careful not to drip). **Bake at 325 for 25-26 minutes** until tops are lightly browned. Cool in pans approx. 15 minutes before carefully removing tartlets to wire racks to cool completely (use the edge of a paring knife to get them out if needed). Best served at room temp.

Makes approx. 45 tartlets (allowing for breakage). Can be stored for several days at room temp. (or frozen) in airtight containers. The tops are very delicate, so only store these in a single layer!

Morning Treats & Other Goodies!

Fresh Blueberry Crumb Cake

Homemade Chocolate Pudding
for Chocolate Cream Pies and Tartlets

Lee's Drinking Man's Custard

Ruth's German Fruit Kuchen

Bards Alley Gingerbread

Orange Blossom Granola

Lemon Dainty

Lemon Pound Cake

Italian Lemon Ricotta Cake

Lee's Pecan Swirl Coffee Cake

Carmela's Amazing Pumpkin Muffins

Fresh Blueberry Crumb Cake

I designed this for Bards Alley Bookstore & Café in Vienna, Virginia, and it was an instant hit! Not too sweet, subtly spiced, bursting with fresh berries. This makes a very large crumb cake – perfect for guests.

Ingredients:

⅔ cup	All-purpose flour (Gold Medal pref.)
⅔ cup, packed, slightly rounded	Domino Light Brown Sugar
6 Tbs. (¾ stick)	Unsalted butter (Land O' Lakes pref.), very soft
¼ tsp., rounded	Cinnamon
3 dashes	Nutmeg
4 cups	All-purpose flour
3 tsps.	Baking powder
1 tsp.	Baking soda
1 tsp.	Salt

½ cup (1 stick)	Unsalted butter, room temp.
1 ⅓ cups	Domino Sugar
2 XL	Eggs, room temp.
2 ½ tsps.	Mexican vanilla
2 cups	Whole buttermilk, shake well before measuring
1 Tbs.	Whole milk
2 cups, rounded	Fresh blueberries, washed, laid to dry
1 Tbs.	All-purpose flour for tossing

Directions: Preheat oven to 350 degrees

1. In a medium bowl, make crumb topping by mixing ⅔ cup of flour and spices with a fork, then adding brown sugar and soft butter. Use a pastry cutter to start, ending with your fingertips to mix well. Topping should be in clumps.

2. Grease a 13x9-inch metal baking pan with Crisco and line with parchment paper. Sift together dry ingredients. In a glass measuring cup, stir together buttermilk, milk, and vanilla.

3. Using a standing mixer with paddle attachment, beat butter until smooth, gradually adding sugar in a steady stream. Cream together on medium-high for 1.5-2 minutes. Scrape bowl, then add eggs one at a time on medium, mixing well after each.

4. Gradually add dry ingredients by large spoonfuls alternately with buttermilk mixture on low, starting and ending with dry ingredients, until just combined. Scrape bowl and mix briefly. Batter will be very thick.

5. Transfer batter into a large mixing bowl; gently fold in flour-tossed berries by hand with a large rubber spatula, being careful not to break any. Gently scoop batter into prepared pan, smoothing the top so that the middle is no thicker than the rest. Crumble topping evenly over entire cake, using all of it.

6. **Bake at 350 for 40 minutes,** then lightly cover with heavy-duty foil and bake an **additional 5 minutes** until golden brown, set in center, and tester comes out clean. Allow cake to cool in pan on wire rack for 3 hours before wrapping with Press'n Seal, then foil. Best served at room temp.

This cake feeds a crowd and will easily yield 15-20 pieces! Can be stored at room temp. for two to three days.

To freeze: wrap individual pieces in plastic, then place them inside airtight containers.

Homemade Chocolate Pudding

for Chocolate Cream Pies and Tartlets

I taught this homemade pudding recipe to middle-schoolers when both of my boys were that age. The students loved it! The pudding is creamy and rich and has a depth of chocolate flavor that can't be beat. It is delicious on its own (very retro!), used as the filling for an amazing Chocolate Cream Pie (my son Nick's #1 favorite), or piped into mini tart shells for parties!

Plan ahead as pudding is best made the day before use in a pie or tartlets.

Can be made the same day if serving as pudding – delicious topped with my Amaretto Whipped Cream!

Ingredients:

2 ½ cups	Whole milk
1 cup, rounded	Nestlé Semi-Sweet Chocolate chips
1 oz.	Baker's Unsweetened Baking Chocolate, chopped
1 oz.	Ghirardelli's Semi-Sweet Chocolate (from bar or chips)
4 XL	Egg yolks
⅔ cup	Domino Sugar
¼ cup	Cornstarch *(reduce to 3 Tbs. if serving as pudding)*
¼ tsp.	Salt
2 tsps.	Mexican vanilla
2 Tbs.	Unsalted butter (Land O'Lakes pref.), cold, cut in half
2 Tbs.	Whole milk, cold

Directions:

Chocolate Pudding:

1. Measure out all ingredients beforehand. Keep butter and 2 Tbs. of finishing milk very cold until ready to use.

2. Scald milk in a heavy-bottomed pot over medium-high heat (tiny bubbles will form around the edge). Carefully swirl the pot several times during this process.

3. In a large bowl, vigorously whisk the egg yolks by hand, add sugar in a steady stream, and continue to whisk until very light in color and thickened. Add cornstarch and salt and whisk until blended.

4. Using a fork, remove any "skin" from surface of scalded milk; add milk a little at a time into egg mixture, whisking constantly. After three to four small additions, continue to slowly whisk in the rest of the milk until fully incorporated.

5. Wash and dry the pot and add pudding base back into it. Whisk over medium heat until thick, being sure to scrape along sides and bottom of pot, until an instant-read thermometer reaches 165 degrees. This may take up to 5 minutes. Turn burner to low and cook for an additional 1 minute (do not skip this step!). Take pudding off the burner and immediately add all chocolates, whisking to melt. Next, add vanilla, then butter one tablespoon at a time, whisking after each. When butter has melted, finish with cold milk to stop the cooking. Scrape along sides and bottom edges of the pot with a large rubber spatula and whisk pudding until smooth.

6. Immediately pour pudding into a glass bowl and cover with plastic wrap, pressing directly onto the top. Chill overnight if using for a pie or tartlets. If serving pudding on its own, allow it to chill for several hours (but taste it warm!).

Chocolate Cream Pie Assembly:

If using pudding for a Chocolate Cream Pie, you can either make it one day ahead as instructed or pour warm custard directly into a pie crust (especially if you are pressed for time!). This can be a pre-baked homemade pie crust or a store-bought one. My family wants their pie in an Oreo Cookie Pie Crust, and that's what they get!

1. If using warm pudding in pie crust, allow chocolate-filled pie to chill in fridge for at least 2 hours (covered with cake dome) before topping it with whipped cream and chilling it for at least another 2 hours before cutting and serving.

2. If using cold pudding, gently loosen with a large rubber spatula and smooth it into pie crust. Immediately top with whipped cream and chill for at least 2 hours before serving.

Mini Chocolate Tartlet Assembly:

The chocolate pudding must be made the day before so that you can successfully pipe it into tartlet shells. I always make my own shells, but that's labor-intensive, and the star of these tartlets is the filling! You can certainly buy high-quality pre-made tartlet shells, pipe the cold chocolate pudding inside, and decorate with homemade stabilized whipped cream. Tres chic!

Notes on whipped cream:
For pies, use Extra Creamy Cool Whip for an easy cheat.
For tartlets, use homemade stabilized whipped cream (recipe found on my Fancy Lemon Tartlet and Mini Key Lime Pie recipes).

To serve as pudding, top with my Amaretto Whipped Cream (recipe found in cake section). Decorate finished pies, tartlets, and individual servings of pudding with chocolate shavings, chocolate curls, or dust with cocoa powder.

Pies, tartlets, and the pudding itself all must be kept cold and served well chilled.

Lee's Drinking Man's Custard

This was one of my mom's specialties. Lee Hessney Pomponio of Arlington, Virginia, was a fabulous cook. She made this often when we were growing up, and everyone in our immediate family has continued the tradition.
Lee called it Drinking Man's, not referring to any booze (there is none), just that it is so good you'll literally want to drink it! Serve this over fresh berries (even fabulous over fresh pineapple). Makes delightful mini "parfaits" for a crowd.

Plan ahead as custard must chill overnight before serving.

Ingredients:

4 cups (1 quart)	Whole milk
4 XL	Eggs, slight room temp.
1 cup	Domino Sugar
1 ½ - 2 tsps.	Mexican vanilla

Directions:

1. Scald milk in a heavy-bottomed pot over medium-high heat (tiny bubbles will form around edge). Carefully swirl the pot several times during this process.

2. In a large bowl, vigorously whisk the eggs by hand, add sugar in a steady stream, and continue to whisk until very light in color and thickened.

3. Using a fork, remove any "skin" from surface of scalded milk; add milk a little at a time into egg mixture, whisking constantly. After three to four small additions, continue to slowly whisk in the rest of the milk until fully incorporated.

4. Wash and dry the pot and add custard base back into it. Using a large rubber spatula, slowly but constantly stir custard over medium heat until thick, traces the back of a wooden spoon (leaves a clear path when you run your finger through it), and reaches 165 degrees on an instant-read thermometer. This could take up to 10 minutes! Be sure to scrape along the sides and bottom of the pot as you are stirring. Be careful: the custard can go from perfect to curdled in a snap!

5. Immediately pour custard into a large glass bowl (it can be poured through a mesh strainer). Cool custard on the counter (2 hours), uncovered. When completely cool, whisk in 1 ½ tsps. of vanilla, taste, and add more as needed. Cover bowl with plastic wrap and chill overnight. Serve cold, ladled over fresh fruit.

Makes 12 regular-size servings. Custard will last three to four days, covered, in fridge (move custard to an airtight container for best results).

Ruth's German Fruit Kuchen

Ruth Alikanian, my dear friend Eva Dempster's mom, was originally from Germany and she was a fabulous cook and baker! I ate many meals at her home as a teenager, and she always made her Blueberry Kuchen for me. Eva is known for her Apfel (apple) version! This German Kuchen is a single layer, rather simple cake – but is absolutely delicious.

Use only the freshest fruit in season for the best taste!

Ingredients:

1 ½ cups	All-purpose flour (Gold Medal pref.)
1 ½ tsps.	Baking powder
⅛ tsp.	Salt
¾ cup (1 ½ sticks)	Unsalted butter (Land O'Lakes pref.), room temp.
1 ½ cups	Domino Sugar
3 XL	Eggs, room temp.
1 tsp.	Mexican vanilla

2 cups	Fresh blueberries, washed, laid out to dry OR
4 to 5	Ripe peaches, peeled, cut into approx. 8 slices each OR
4 to 5	Ripe black plums, cut into approx. 8 slices each

Directions: **Preheat oven to 350 degrees**

1. Grease a 10-inch springform pan with Crisco, line bottom with a parchment paper round, and dust sides with flour. Sift together dry ingredients (note: I add ¼ tsp. of nutmeg to the dry ingredients before sifting for the peach version).

2. Using a standing mixer with paddle attachment, beat butter until smooth, gradually adding sugar in a steady stream. Cream together on medium-high until light and fluffy. Scrape bowl, then add eggs one at a time on medium, mixing well after each. Add vanilla.

3. Gradually add in dry ingredients by large spoonfuls with mixer on low, beating until just combined. Scrape bowl and mix briefly. Scoop batter into prepared pan, smoothing the top gently with a large rubber spatula. Top with fresh fruit as follows:

Blueberry Kuchen: Toss berries with 1 ½ Tbs. sugar, ½ Tbs. cornstarch and ½ tsp. vanilla.

Peach Kuchen: Use fresh local peaches if you can! Peel, core, and slice peaches and toss with sugar, cornstarch, and vanilla as described above. Press slices gently into the batter in a pretty pattern.

Plum Kuchen: Core and slice black plums and toss with sugar, cornstarch, and vanilla as described above; add a dash of cardamom. Press slices gently into the batter in a pretty pattern; sprinkle with more sugar if plums are tart.

4. **Bake at 350 for 45 minutes,** cover lightly with heavy-duty foil, and **bake an additional 5-10 minutes** until the center is set. Let cool completely in pan on a wire rack (2 hours); wrap with Press'n Seal, then foil. Best served at room temp.

Yields 10-12 slices. Can be stored at room temp. for two to three days.
Can be frozen if well wrapped.

Bards Alley Gingerbread

Designed for the café at Bards Alley Bookstore! Simple, moist, not too sweet, with just the right balance of spice. Perfect in the morning or for a little special treat any time of day. This recipe makes two lovely loaves.

Ingredients:

2 cups	All-purpose flour (Gold Medal pref.)
1 tsp.	Baking soda
1 ½ tsps., slightly rounded	Ginger
¾ tsp., slightly rounded	Nutmeg
¾ tsp., slightly rounded	Cinnamon
½ tsp., slightly rounded	Cloves
½ tsp.	Salt

½ cup (1 stick)	Unsalted butter (Land O'Lakes pref.), room temp.
¼ cup	Domino Sugar
¼ cup, packed, slightly rounded	Domino Dark Brown Sugar
½ cup	Grandma's Original Molasses (not Robust)
1 tsp.	Mexican vanilla
2 XL	Eggs, room temp.
1 cup	Whole buttermilk, shake well before measuring

Directions: **Preheat oven to 340 degrees**

1. Grease two light-colored metal loaf pans liberally with Crisco. Sift together dry ingredients. Measure molasses in a lightly oiled glass measuring cup.

2. Using a standing mixer with paddle attachment, beat butter until smooth, add both sugars, then cream together on medium-high until fluffy and well combined. Add molasses and vanilla on low, scrape bowl, and mix well. Add eggs one at a time on medium, mixing well after each.

3. Gradually add dry ingredients by large spoonfuls alternately with buttermilk on low, starting and ending with dry ingredients, until just combined. Scrape bowl and mix briefly. Pour batter into prepared pans, weighing each on a food scale for even distribution. Smooth top of batter and make a seam down the center with a large rubber spatula.

4. **Bake at 340 for 40 minutes**, then lay heavy-duty foil over top and bake for an **additional 12-14 minutes** until tester comes out clean. Let pans cool on wire racks for 13 minutes, then gently flip cakes out to cool completely. Allow cakes to finish cooling (2 hours) before wrapping with plastic, then foil. Best served at room temp.

Each loaf yields 10 slices. Can be stored at room temp. two to three days (or frozen) if well wrapped.

Orange Blossom Granola

Super flavorful, easy to make, and much more economical than buying it! Great over berries and yogurt. Add white or dark chocolate chips or yogurt-covered raisins once granola has cooled for a little sweeter treat. This recipe makes a lot of granola – perfect for gifting!

Ingredients:

2 cups, rounded	Old-fashioned rolled oats (do not use steel-cut or instant)
½ cup	Raw pumpkin seeds
1 ¼ cups	Unsweetened coconut, large flakes (found on healthy snack aisle)
1 cup, rounded	Raw walnuts, roughly chopped
½ cup	Orange blossom honey
1 Large	Orange, juiced
2 Tbs.	Unsalted butter (Land O'Lakes pref.), optional
2 Tbs., slightly rounded	Crystallized ginger, finely chopped
½ tsp.	Fine sea salt (if avail. - regular salt if not)
1 tsp., slightly rounded	Cinnamon
2 dashes	Nutmeg
½ cup	Dried fruit of choice (golden raisins, dates, cherries, or cranberries)

Directions: **Preheat oven to 350 degrees**

1. Line a large baking sheet with parchment paper. Mix oats, pumpkin seeds, coconut flakes, and walnuts on prepared pan and **bake at 350 for 10 minutes**, stirring occasionally, until lightly browned.

2. While the mixture is baking, combine honey, orange juice, and butter (if using) in a small pot and cook on low until butter melts and mixture bubbles slightly. Remove from heat and whisk in ginger, salt, and spices. Set aside to cool slightly.

3. Remove oat mixture from oven and scoop it into a large bowl. Combine this with the honey syrup and ½ cup of dried fruit and stir with a large rubber spatula until well mixed. Place granola back onto parchment-lined pan, spreading out evenly.

4. **Lower oven to 300 degrees and bake undisturbed for 15 minutes.** Cool granola completely on pan, then divide into jars or plastic containers.

If using butter, granola must be stored in fridge. If not, it can be stored at room temp. in airtight containers.

Lemon Dainty

This is a wonderful old-time dessert, also referred to as a pudding cake. When cooked, it separates into two layers: cake on top, delicate pudding/sauce on the bottom. Very easy to make, but always impressive to serve! Perfect when paired with fresh blueberries. You'll need lots of large juicy lemons for this one!

Ingredients:

1 cup	Domino Sugar
¼ cup	All-purpose flour (Gold Medal pref.)
⅛ tsp.	Salt
2 Tbs.	Unsalted butter (Land O'Lakes pref.), melted
5 Tbs.	Fresh lemon juice
2 Small	Lemons for zesting
3 XL	Eggs, room temp., separated just before using
1 ½ cups	Whole milk
Extra	Butter, very soft

Directions: **Preheat oven to 350 degrees**

1. Chill bowl and whisk attachment of a standing mixer in freezer. Liberally butter a 1.5-quart glass casserole or souffle dish. Boil water for a "bain-marie" (water bath).

2. In a large bowl, mix sugar, flour, and salt with a fork. Add melted butter, lemon juice, and zest and whisk vigorously by hand until blended. Add egg yolks and milk and whisk until smooth.

3. In the chilled mixing bowl, beat egg whites with whisk attachment on medium-high until stiff peaks form (do not overbeat!). Then, using a large rubber spatula, fold this into the lemon base in 2 - 3 additions until fully incorporated.

4. Pour batter into prepared dish; set dish into a large metal roasting pan and carefully fill pan with 1-inch of hot water creating the bain-marie.

5. **Bake at 350 for 35 minutes,** then lay a piece of heavy-duty foil carefully over the top and **bake an additional 10 minutes**. Dainty should be puffed, still a bit jiggly, and nicely browned. Remove roasting pan from oven but allow glass dish to remain in the water bath, uncovered, for an additional 5 minutes.

6. Carefully remove glass dish to a wire rack to cool. Dainty can be served slightly warm, at room temp., or chilled. Always store the Dainty, covered, in the fridge.

Makes approx. 8 servings. Can be made one day ahead if serving cold. Recipe can be doubled for a large souffle dish. Bake on 2nd rack from bottom in 350 oven for a total of 60 minutes, lightly covering with foil after 40 minutes.

Lemon Pound Cake

I developed this recipe for the café at Bards Alley Bookstore. Very moist, with a bright lemon flavor. The lemon syrup and lemon icing make a big difference! This makes two lovely loaves.

Ingredients:

4 cups	All-purpose flour (Gold Medal pref.)
¾ tsp.	Baking soda
¼ tsp.	Baking powder
¾ tsp.	Salt
1 ⅓ cups (2 sticks + 5 ⅓ Tbs.)	Unsalted butter (Land O'Lakes pref.), room temp.
3 cups	Domino Sugar
4 XL	Eggs, room temp.
6 Tbs.	Fresh lemon juice
2 Large	Lemons for zesting
1 ½ tsps.	Mexican vanilla
1 ½ cups	Whole buttermilk, shake well before measuring

Directions:

1. Combine buttermilk, zest, juice, and vanilla, and let steep together for 45 minutes.

2. Grease two light-colored metal loaf pans liberally with Crisco, line with parchment paper on bottom and up sides; smooth out creases. Sift together dry ingredients.

3. Using a standing mixer with paddle attachment, beat butter until smooth, gradually adding sugar in a steady stream. Cream together on medium for 4 minutes. Scrape bowl, then add eggs one at a time on medium, mixing well after each.

4. Gradually add dry ingredients by large spoonfuls alternately with buttermilk mixture on low, starting and ending with dry ingredients. Scrape bowl and continue to mix on low until smooth, taking care not to overbeat. Pour batter into prepared pans, weighing each on a food scale for even distribution. Smooth top of batter and make a seam down the center with a large rubber spatula.

5. **Bake at 325 for 55-60 minutes** until tester comes out clean. Do not overbake!
   While cakes are baking, make lemon syrup and lemon icing (recipes below).

6. Let cakes cool in pans 10 minutes; use the parchment paper to carefully lift them up and out of the pans. Place cakes directly onto wire racks, peel paper away from the sides, and lay wax paper underneath each rack.

7. Immediately glaze with hot lemon syrup (2 - 3 passes with a pastry brush). Cool cakes 1 hour, then glaze with lemon icing, allowing it to drip down the sides. Allow cakes to cool an additional hour before placing them onto a flat plate or cake board. Wrap the sides carefully with plastic wrap and store them under a cake dome (or tent with foil). Best served at room temp.

Finishing Syrup and Icing:

Lemon Syrup:

¼ cup water + ¼ cup granulated sugar, brought to boil for 1-2 minutes until sugar dissolves. Add 1 ½ Tbs. fresh lemon juice. Stir until combined. Use hot syrup on warm cakes.

Lemon Icing:

1 ⅓ cups confectioners sugar, sifted, whisked with 3 ⅓ Tbs. fresh lemon juice and ⅓ tsp. lemon oil. Use icing immediately to glaze partially cooled cakes.

Each loaf yields 10 slices. Can be stored at room temp. for two to three days.
Can be frozen if well wrapped.

Italian Lemon Ricotta Cake

A wonderfully light lemon cake....great for the morning, afternoon, or evening! This is a very moist cake, simple to make, but different enough to have a certain "wow" factor!

Ingredients:

1 ½ cups	All-purpose flour (Gold Medal pref.)
½ tsp.	Baking soda
½ tsp.	Salt
¾ cup (1 ½ sticks)	Unsalted butter (Land O'Lakes pref.), room temp.
1 ½ cups	Domino Sugar
3 XL	Eggs, room temp.
1 ½ Large	Lemons for zesting
3 Tbs.	Fresh lemon juice
1 tsp.	Mexican vanilla
15 oz. (1 cont.)	Whole milk ricotta cheese (Galbani or Polly-O pref.)

Directions: **Preheat oven to 350 degrees**

1. Grease a 10-inch springform pan with Crisco, cut a parchment paper round to line the bottom, and dust sides with cake flour. Sift together dry ingredients.

2. Using a standing mixer with paddle attachment, beat butter until smooth, gradually adding sugar in a steady stream; add zest. Cream together on medium-high until well combined and light in color. Scrape bowl, add ricotta, and blend on medium-low until light and fluffy (a full 5 minutes).

3. Add eggs one at a time on low, mixing well after each; add vanilla and lemon juice (batter might look slightly curdled). Scrape bowl and mix briefly.

4. Gradually add in dry ingredients by large spoonfuls on low, scrape sides and bottom of bowl, and mix batter for an additional 10 seconds. Pour batter into prepared pan, gently smoothing the top with a large rubber spatula.

5. **Bake at 350 for 38-40 minutes** until tester comes out clean, and top is golden. Let cake cool in pan on wire rack for 15 minutes, then remove the pan collar. Allow cake to cool completely (1.5 hours), then place under a cake dome. Dust with confectioners sugar (through a fine-mesh strainer) just before serving. Best served at room temp.

Yields approx. 12 slices. Can be stored at room temp. for two to three days or in fridge for up to four days.

Freezing is not recommended.

Lee's Pecan Swirl Coffee Cake

One of Lee Hessney Pomponio's (my mother!) famous recipes! She baked this often for us. I introduced it to the café at Bards Alley Bookstore, and it was an instant hit. A very moist coffee cake with an interior swirl of cinnamon-sugared pecans.

Ingredients:

1 tsp., slightly rounded	Cinnamon
½ cup	Domino Sugar
½ cup, slightly rounded	Whole pecans (measure first, then chop)
2 cups	All-purpose flour (Gold Medal pref.)
1 tsp.	Baking powder
1 tsp.	Baking soda
¼ tsp.	Salt
1 cup, slightly rounded	Regular sour cream (Breakstone's or similar), slight room temp.
½ cup (1 stick)	Unsalted butter (Land O'Lakes pref.), room temp.

1 cup	Sugar
2 XL	Eggs, room temp.
1 tsp.	Mexican vanilla

Directions: **Preheat oven to 350 degrees**

1. In a small bowl, mix cinnamon and sugar with a fork. Place whole nuts on a plate and discard any with dark spots or shells. In a food processor with metal insert, pulse whole pecans until somewhat fine (a few small pieces are ok). Add nuts to cinnamon sugar and mix well.

2. Liberally and thoroughly grease a 10-inch Bundt pan with Crisco; sprinkle a little bit of the nut mixture into pan. Sift together dry ingredients.

3. Using a standing mixer with paddle attachment, beat butter until smooth, gradually adding sugar in a steady stream. Cream together on medium for 3 minutes until light in color and very smooth. Scrape bowl, then add eggs one at a time on low, mixing well after each; add vanilla.

4. Gradually add dry ingredients by large spoonfuls alternately with sour cream on low, starting and ending with dry ingredients. Scrape bowl and mix on low for 3 minutes. Spoon half of the batter into prepared pan; sprinkle on most of the nut mixture, reserving approx. 3 Tbs. Spoon remaining batter on top of the nuts, smoothing out the top. Sprinkle about 1 ½ Tbs. of nut mixture as final layer.

5. **Bake at 350 for 40 minutes**, then cover lightly with a piece of heavy-duty foil and bake an **additional 5 minutes** until golden and tester comes out clean. Cool pan on wire rack for precisely 15 minutes, then turn pan upside down on rack, giving a good shake until cake releases. Immediately sprinkle top of warm cake with remaining nuts. Cool cake completely (2 hours) before wrapping. Best served at room temp.

Yields 14-16 pieces. Can be stored for two to three days at room temp. (or frozen) if well wrapped.

Carmela's Amazing Pumpkin Muffins

Adapted from my friend Carmela Westcott's original recipe. Perfectly moist, high-domed muffins, not overly sweet - and they freeze beautifully!

Ingredients:

¼ cup (½ stick)	Unsalted butter (Land O'Lakes pref.)
¼ cup, slightly rounded	Crisco Vegetable Shortening
1 ¾ cups	All-purpose flour (Gold Medal pref.)
1 tsp.	Baking soda
½ tsp.	Salt
1 cup, level	Domino Sugar
½ cup, packed, slightly rounded	Domino Light Brown Sugar
2 tsps., slightly rounded	Cinnamon

⅓ tsp.	Nutmeg
2 XL (or Jumbo)	Eggs, room temp.
1 15 oz. can	Libby's Pure Pumpkin
1 Large	Orange for zesting
1 tsp.	Mexican vanilla
⅓ cup	Chopped walnuts (optional) *Or*
⅓ cup	Golden raisins (optional)

Directions: **Preheat oven to 400 degrees, then bake at 375**

1. In a small pot, melt butter and Crisco together on low, then set aside to cool. In a large bowl, whisk together by hand all dry ingredients, both sugars, and spices.

2. In a separate bowl, whisk the eggs vigorously by hand, then add in the pumpkin, melted butter/ Crisco mixture, orange zest, and vanilla. Pour wet ingredients into the dry ingredients and stir gently with a large rubber spatula until just incorporated. Do not overmix! Fold in nuts or raisins if using.

3. Liberally spray regular-size muffin pans with Pam for Baking, being sure to get a little on the pan's top surface. Then, with a large serving spoon, scoop batter into each tin filling to the top; add a second small dome of batter on top of that (essentially over-filling).

4. Place muffin pans inside of a 400-degree oven then immediately adjust heat down to 375 degrees. **Bake at 375 for 23-25 minutes** until just set in the middle and tester comes out clean. Allow pans to cool on wire racks until you can safely tilt or lift out each muffin. Then allow them to cool completely, dome side down, on wire racks. Best served at room temp.

Makes 9 large muffins. Can be stored at room temp. for two to three days (or frozen) in airtight containers.

All You Need is Love & a Little Something Sweet

Luscious Coconut Cupcakes

Peanut Butter Chocolate Cupcakes

Pumpkin Spice Cupcakes

Fancy Lemon Tartlets

Chocolate Frangelico Crinkles

All desserts were handma...

Mary Lee's Des...

Mary Lee's Preferred Brands

If you want to replicate my desserts exactly as I make them, here's your "cheat sheet" for the products I swear by!

- Gold Medal All-Purpose Flour
  (Top-rated non-organic flour by
  Epicurious, February 2018)

- Softasilk or Swans Down Cake Flour

- Domino Pure Cane Sugar
  (Sold as C&H on West Coast)

- Domino Confectioners (Powdered) Sugar

- Domino Dark Brown Sugar

- Domino Light Brown Sugar

- Land O'Lakes Unsalted Butter

- Crisco All-Vegetable Shortening
  (In a can, not sticks)

- Wesson Pure Vegetable Oil

- Skippy Regular Creamy Peanut Butter
  (Do not use reduced-fat or all-natural)

- Hershey's Cocoa Powder

- Nestlé Toll House Semi-Sweet
  Chocolate Morsels
  (Referred to as chips in this book)

- Nestlé Toll House Premier White Morsels
  (Referred to as chips in this book)

- Ghirardelli Semi-Sweet Chocolate Chips

- Ghirardelli Semi-Sweet Chocolate
  Baking Bar

- Baker's Unsweetened Chocolate
  Baking Bar

- Baker's German's Sweet Chocolate
  Baking Bar

- Breakstone's Regular All-Natural
  Sour Cream
  (Do not use reduced-fat)

- Philadelphia Regular Original Cream Cheese
  (Do not use reduced-fat)

- Mexican Vanilla – any high-quality brand
  (I use Orlando Vanilla from Mexico, but
  it's hard to find!)

- Nielsen-Massey Pure Almond Extract
  (I've tested several: this is by far the best -
  not bitter - smooth, with floral notes)

- McCormick: Pure Lemon, Pure Orange,
  Coconut, Pure Mint, Pure Peppermint
  Extracts

- Simply Organic Lemon Oil

- Simply Organic ground spices

- Rumford Baking Powder

- Arm & Hammer Pure Baking Soda

- Morton's Iodized Table Salt
  (Do not use Kosher or Sea Salt)

- Libby's Pure Pumpkin

- Baker's Angel Flake Sweetened Coconut

- Thai Kitchen Organic Coconut Milk
  (Do not use "Lite")

- PET Evaporated Milk

- Eagle Brand Sweetened Condensed Milk

- Karo Light Corn Syrup

About the Author

Mary Lee Montfort started baking as a pantry and line cook at the Union Bay Café in Seattle, Washington, in 1993, under Chef and Owner Mark Manley, where his homemade desserts were part of her responsibility. Mary Lee loved working for Chef Manley and the energy and pace of working "on the line" during the dinner service. Making desserts was more evenly paced during the quiet part of the day, where she learned so much about baking. In 2004, Mary Lee took her two-year Union Bay Café experience and started Mary Lee's Desserts in Vienna, Virginia.

Mary Lee was lucky enough to have caught the attention of restaurant critic and writer David Hagedorn. As a food columnist for The Washington Post, David included Mary Lee in an article in 2007 that featured two of her cakes - her Pumpkin Spice Cake and her spectacular Peanut Butter Chocolate Cake. Then in December 2011, two of Mary Lee's cookie recipes were featured in The Post's Annual Holiday Cookie Issue: Chocolate Frangelico Crinkles and M&M Bars. Her M&M Bar recipe became the single most viewed and downloaded recipe in The Post for all of 2012. The Post re-published that recipe in November 2020.

In the fall of 2012, Mr. Hagedorn launched the Chefs for Equality Gala, a fundraising event for the Human Rights Campaign, which brought together top chefs and mixologists from all over the Washington D.C. region. David asked Mary Lee to bake for their guests' swag bags, which she did that inaugural year and for many years after. Mary Lee will tell you that it was the honor of her career to participate in this way, supporting marriage equality and the LGBTQ community, among the best in the food business.

In 2017, Jennifer Morrow asked Mary Lee to bake a weekly cake for her brand-new indie bookstore, Bards Alley Bookstore & Café, in the heart of Vienna. That one cake soon turned into an abundance of weekly cupcakes, cookies, bars, and specialty morning treats, many designed just for the café. Mary Lee baked for Bards Alley for nearly two years, and she was thrilled to have her desserts available in retail.

Mary Lee ran Mary Lee's Desserts as a fully licensed home-based baking business from 2004 to 2019. Desserts were always made to order for every customer by Mary Lee, which quickly set her apart from commercial bakeries. From single cakes to large corporate events, holidays – when Mary Lee routinely baked over 1,000 cookies – to galas and Bards Alley, her desserts were always known for their quality and delicious taste. Mary Lee is now a cookbook author whose book sales benefit charitable organizations.

Recipe Index